The
Assessment
Bridge

Friends. Copyright © 2000 by Hilda Epner. Reprinted by permission.

The Assessment Bridge

Positive Ways to Link
Tests to Learning, Standards,
and Curriculum Improvement

Pearl G. Solomon

CORWIN PRESS, INC.
A Sage Publications Company
Thousand Oaks, California

For information:

Corwin Press, Inc.
Sage Publications Company
2455 Teller Road
Thousand Oaks, California 91320
www.corwinpress.com

Sage Publications Ltd.
6 Bonhill Street
London EC2A 4PU United Kingdom

Sage Publications India Pvt. Ltd.
M-32 Market
Greater Kailash I
New Delhi 110 048 India

Printed in the United States of America

Library of Congress Cataloging-in-Publication Data

Solomon, Pearl G. (Pearl Gold), 1929-
  The assessment bridge: Positive ways to link tests to learning, standards, and curriculum improvement / by Pearl G. Solomon.
      p. cm.
Includes bibliographical references and index.
  ISBN 0-7619-4593-8 (c) -- ISBN 0-7619-4594-6 (p)
  1. Educational tests and measurements--United States.
  2. Education--Curricula--Standards--United States. I. Title.
  LB3051 .S63 2002
  371.26´4--dc21

                                            2002002767

This book is printed on acid-free paper.

02 03 04 05 06 07 7 6 5 4 3 2 1

Acquisitions Editor:	Faye Zucker
Editorial Assistant:	Julia Parnell
Production Editor:	Olivia Weber
Typesetter/Designer:	Siva Math Setters, Chennai, India
Cover Designer:	Michael Dubowe
Production Artist:	Janet Foulger

Contents

Foreword

Bridges make it possible for people to cross narrow streams or raging waters, apt metaphors for the issues and problems that confront today's teachers, professors, and school administrators as they strive to link curriculum, assessment, and the problems of school change and school renewal. In the case of *The Assessment Bridge: Positive Ways to Link Tests to Learning, Standards, and Curriculum Improvement,* author Pearl Solomon becomes the guide who accompanies us on our voyage from one land mass to the next.

Conversational in manner, yet deeply thought out, Solomon's book offers us her personal experience in developing a comprehensive program that uses testing, a changed curriculum, and the necessary supportive conditions to ensure implementation. But that is not all Solomon offers us: Solidly undergirding our bridge's roadway are the necessary research and historical context to help us understand not only why we are embarked on the journey of school reform but also how to think about our journey, learn from it, develop it, and become its leaders.

By reading this book, we learn about the context of 21st-century education. We learn why accountability, standards, and high-stakes tests have become part of the landscape on both sides of our bridge. We learn the vocabulary of testing, the means to restructure curriculum, and—a necessary prerequisite for building bridges—the many ways to develop leadership.

The Assessment Bridge uses four major components to span the gaps between testing, curriculum, and change, and together those turn this book into a unified roadmap for school reform: building capacity, generating ownership, developing leadership, and providing time for learning and change. By taking us by the hand and teaching us how to look at the context within which we live (and how that context keeps changing), we come to a better understanding of how we might *embrace* testing. We come to see testing not as a narrowing of the curriculum, but as a means to deepen teachers' involvement in creating the important ideas that must be assessed so that teachers can create curriculum and instruction appropriate for their students.

By providing multiple entry points onto the bridge between testing and curriculum, Solomon shows us that we can start with standards or we can start with tests, but none of us has to fall into the trap of being just an assessment person, or just a content person, or just a change person. Encyclopedic in its detail, yet always human, accessible, and friendly, Pearl Solomon's book is just the kind of bridge we need to span the ideological wars and make schools work for teachers and their students.

Ann Lieberman
Senior Scholar, Carnegie Foundation
for the Advancement of Teaching
Visiting Professor, Stanford University

Preface

WHAT THIS BOOK IS ABOUT
AND WHO SHOULD READ IT

This book is a response to one of the front-page items in every newspaper today, the looming crisis in our nation's schools and the suggested remedy for the crisis, state-mandated and distally developed tests: tests designed far away from the teachers and children they measure. Written tests are just one form of the many measures or assessments that play an important part in the learning-teaching process. Imagined as the only way to ensure success and uniformity in an increasingly diverging and world-dependent society, the tests have become a hurdle for students, parents, teachers, and schools to overcome. Fortunately, human beings are blessed with the ability to overcome hurdles; usually, the process of overcoming them makes us stronger and wiser.

Geographical obstacles to distant but promising resources have been overcome with human ingenuity and energy by building bridges. Bridges have useful functions, but, additionally, they are, in themselves, often objects of beauty. This book offers suggestions for building a bridge to overcome the testing hurdle and, perhaps, in the process, building a better educational structure of function and beauty.

Every bridge has a crossover goal and a starting and ending place. My crossover goal is to bring understanding, coping skills, and possible value to the current headlong thrust into an educational culture governed by mandated tests. My bridge will offer neither outright condemnation nor unconditional support for this trend but will accept the tests as reality, a reality that educators have to contend with as part of the terrain. The trend is an obstacle that, perhaps, can be overcome with new and better connections between what educators believe is best and what they do for children, parents, and society—and how society measures and supports what they do.

The broader problem analyses and suggestions for resolution presented are intended for all the related decision makers, including the politicians and government officials who mandate that tests must be given, as the only solution to our nation's problem of underachieving groups of students. The specifics of the remedies may prove most useful for those who wish to confront them in the most productive way—our teachers and curriculum leaders.

AN OUTLINE OF THE BRIDGE-BUILDING STEPS

My starting place in Chapter 1 begins, like the bridge engineer, with an attempt to define the problem. A broad view of the terrain is a good place to begin. Understanding and knowledge of history, as we will see ahead, is an important variable in affecting school change. It places the present in context and avoids repeating actions that have previously had negative results. It provides a baseline for recognizing critical changes that must be dealt with. Sometimes, it may also offer suggestions that have been successful in the past. Chapter 2 hones in on the more current setting, the existing framework and current specifics of the problem, and then it reviews and evaluates a sample of already tried or proposed resolutions for improving schools. The purpose of this is to learn and gather the very best materials and actions, make any needed minor adjustments to those that have promise, and discard the hopeless ones.

Following the diagnosis of obstacles to overcome, Chapter 3 reviews the clustered variables of history, vision, ownership, capacity, leadership, and time, which are embedded in the process of changing schools and must be reckoned with. Having already begun to address the variables of history and vision in previous chapters, I will suggest some of the first steps in building capacity, generating ownership, and providing leadership and time. Each of these is then pursued in greater depth in the following chapters.

One advantage for the bridge builder is the availability of local materials. If there is good local sand for concrete, use it. Chapter 4 will present my overall vision of how distally produced tests, generated far from the students they measure, can fit into the overall role of assessment as a guide to instruction. It will suggest how schools and teachers can build their capacity to use high-stakes, standards-based tests, in conjunction with their own proximal classroom or locally developed measures, as a guideline for making needed changes in curriculum and instructional practices. There will be specific suggestions for how educators can use rubrics and the disaggregated analyses of their own and distal tests to identify areas of greatest need. Disaggregation can also be helpful in identifying affecting variables such as socioeconomic status and gender, as well as environmental variables such as class size and teachers' attitudes. Knowing what these variables are can help us focus our energies so that they will have the maximum effect.

Chapter 5 will outline a process for building consensus on the specifics of the school's curriculum, as well as its relationship to diagnosed needs. It presents two alternative design processes, beginning either with the mandated tests or with the curriculum standards upon which the tests are based. Engagement of teachers in the process of designing need-responsive curriculum can bring them a sense of order and purpose that may serve to ease their existing anxiety and build ownership.

Chapters 6 and 7 lead to the ending place for my bridge: better schools. Just as the engineer depends on a crew of competent builders, the success of our schools and our children depends on good teaching, parenting, and leadership. It also depends on having children ready to learn. Chapter 6 presents a model for recruiting teachers, building their capacity, and nurturing them through the tough beginning years. The model is based on an analysis of our urgent need for capable teachers, and it offers specific suggestions for meeting the need for both new and newly capable incumbent teachers.

Chapter 7 addresses the role of leadership in bringing it all together and facilitating successful access to the other side. The critical component of power and its manifestation in the actions of pressure and support are addressed and compared in different educational leadership roles. Alternative models of leadership are presented that address the need for cohesion and the complications and advantages of sharing responsibilities.

SOME IMPORTANT HELPERS

While trying to crystallize concepts from my own prior experience in order to conjoin them with the thinking and actions of others and place them in the current situational context—a constructivist activity—I reflected on the impact of so many others in framing this experience. I need to begin (as I will ahead) with my own teachers, one of whom was particularly inspiring in getting me to think about the school change process and who encouraged me to write. Ann Lieberman is busy inspiring many others, as well, and I am most grateful that she found the time to write a foreword for this book. I then need to thank my many colleagues in the Pearl River, New York, school district with whom I spent 23 years as a teacher and administrator, and who provided many of the examples I used to illustrate my ideas.

Dr. Margaret Fitzpatrick, President of St. Thomas Aquinas College, where I have spent almost 11 years, has been a consistent and enthusiastic supporter of the Marie Curie Math and Science Center and its far-reaching endeavors. She has also conveyed the level of personal confidence in my enterprises that one needs to plunge ahead. My colleagues throughout the college have been similarly supportive, as have the teachers and administrators in the East Ramapo, New York, schools with whom I am presently working so closely. Most of all, I wish to thank my many students, ranging from the 9- and 10-year-olds who sat in my class over 50 years ago to the over-50 career changer who was there this past semester.

There are also individuals in my personal life who deserve recognition. My friends and walking partners, Diana Siegel and Hilda Epner, both teachers, listen to my ideas as we walk, and they respond from their own considerable experience. Hilda is also the artist responsible for the drawings of the frontispiece and epilogue. Keeping me well informed of the vocabulary, values, and actions of the newest generation of learners as we drive home from school each day are my two grandsons, Joseph and Edward Burke, and their car pool companions. My husband, Mel, is always there to support my endeavors and share the time they require. The staff of Corwin Press, and, especially, Executive Editor, Faye Zucker, continue to be wonderful to work with, and I appreciate their confidence, patience, and expertise. It is always rewarding for authors to have someone read their work with a careful, meaningful, and responsive eye. Copy editor Hawley Roddick and production editor Olivia Weber not only did this but also read with such great precision and knowledge that there is no doubt in my mind that this is a far, far better work as a result of their efforts. We all should be grateful for their dedication to a task so well done.

About the Author

Pearl G. Solomon is Professor Emeritus of Teacher Education at St. Thomas Aquinas College in Sparkill, New York. She received a doctorate in educational administration from Teachers College, Columbia University. She has served as a teacher, school administrator, director and officer for professional organizations, and consultant to many school districts, including New York City and Chicago as well as the New York State Education Department and the United States Department of Education. She is the recipient of a number of special awards from the state and community for her work in science, math, health, and career education.

Recent activities include directing the Marie Curie Mathematics and Science Center and its Project McExtend network of teachers in two New York counties. Eisenhower, Goals 2000, and National Science Foundation grants that she authored have enabled large-scale in-service teacher training efforts as well as Saturday enrichment programs in math and science for 5th- through 12th-grade students. Her teaching assignments include graduate courses in curriculum, and math and science methods.

She is a frequent speaker at professional conferences and is the author of several books published by Corwin Press, including *No Small Feat: Taking Time for Change* (1995); *The Curriculum Bridge: From Standards to Actual Classroom Practice* (1998), which was named a *Choice* Outstanding Academic Title; and *The Math We Need to "Know" and "Do": Content Standards for Elementary and Middle Grades* (2000), which was selected as a finalist for Outstanding Writing Award from the American Association of Colleges of Teacher Education.

1 Defining the Problem: The Historical Context

ABOUT THIS CHAPTER

A good starting place for meeting any challenge is to define the problem that must be overcome. The definitions of human problems need to be placed in the context of time, place, and human needs. History frames the present context of each of these in significant ways. A logical framework, therefore, for defining the problems facing the education of students in the United States at the beginning of the 21st century is to review the historical context so that we may better understand the present. My personal vantage point for viewing the terrain of history is somewhat privileged. It is based on 15 years as a student, followed by another 52 years as a student and educator. Because my connection to formal education began in a rural, one-room schoolhouse—not very different from the way it had been in the 19th century—and continues with my present role as a teacher-educator, this personal perspective, in essence, spans 3 centuries. As a bridge builder, I believe this perspective will be useful in defining the problem and in suggesting solutions.

This chapter is not, however, intended as a complete history of education. Other whole texts do this well. It is, instead, meant to be a general and personally selective baseline for making connections to the present that I will present throughout the following chapters.

SCHOOLS AS TRANSMITTERS OF CULTURE

An astronaut returning from a 20-year sojourn in space early in 2001 might have been surprised at what seemed foremost on the minds of Americans—at least as judged by our media and politicians. Instead of exciting reports of progress and thinking about the new frontiers of space, front-page headlines, major articles, and campaign speeches lamented the problems and deficiencies of our educational systems. Well, we do need schools to produce astronauts and scientists and, of course, politicians. Our astronaut shouldn't be too surprised. The other headlines reveal a continuing pattern of a world troubled by conflict: the Balkans, the Middle East, Africa, Southeast Asia, and China, to name just a few; and as I write this book later in the same year, the threat of world terrorism has become reality as the U.S. homeland is struck by surprise with a devastating attack. Cultural differences are often the seeds of conflict.

Education is about transmitting the culture. Public education in this country is also about closing cultural gaps—gaps that many fear as potential sources of human conflict. But why all the interest at this moment in time? As soon as September 23, 2001, 12 days after the attack on this country, Congress was grappling with and making decisions on President George W. Bush's education plan (Associated Press, 2001).

On October 10, 2001, 3 days after the country's attack on Afghanistan, 16 state governors were meeting at an IBM center in Palisades, New York, for the fourth education summit. The location is about 5 minutes from where I teach, but I was not invited, and neither was a fair representation of other teachers and principals. President Bush was supposed to be there but did not appear, and neither did nine other governors who had originally agreed to come. Michigan Governor John Engler gave the rationale for their presence in these dire times, arguing that American strength can only be maintained with an educated population.

"We're in a war," he said. "We want to secure ourselves from enemies internal and external. Ignorance, lack of knowledge, poorly developed skills, these are the kind of internal enemies we can do something about" (Wilson & Weiner, 2001, p. 1B).

A major agenda for the 2001 conference was the problem of the ever-widening gap in test scores between white and minority students. The solution offered by President Bush and supported by both houses of Congress was annual tests for student in Grades 3 to 8. Many state representatives were concerned about the cost of the tests. Rhode Island's commissioner of education Peter McWalters cited a cost of $4 million and expressed concern that the expense would divert dollars from other needs. IBM chairman Lou Gerstner suggested another costly solution to the problem—increasing the salary of teachers (Steinberg, 2001).

The final legislation, passed overwhelmingly by Congress and signed by President Bush in December 2001, mandated his suggestion for federally developed tests in Grades 3 to 8 by 2005 to 2006. It also increased federal funding for 2002 to more than $22.1 billion for America's elementary and secondary schools—a 27% increase over 2001 and a 49% increase over 2000 levels. New directions for federal dollars included funds for private tutoring and within-district school transfer rights for children in failing schools, specific recommendations for the teaching of reading, and more money for charter schools and for training teachers. Greater flexibility for schools in how federal funds are spent might even include expenditures for higher teacher salaries (www.whitehouse.gov/infocus/education/, retrieved January 19, 2002). The questions remain unanswered. Can we make our schools better with this new federal initiative and funding? Are the problems of American education as serious as the critics make them appear? Are the proposed solutions valid? What do the educators think?

History tells us that the degree of public concern with education has varied through time. As far back as the Egyptians, Greeks, and Romans—and considering, as well, the carefully prescribed ritual training of youth in tribal societies—formal schooling has been the hallmark of stable human communities. It is, however, a reciprocal relationship: formal education connoting existing stability but also bearing the responsibility for maintaining it. It is not surprising, then, that in relatively peaceful times, positive public attention is drawn to how we educate our youth and to what we teach them. Interest in education grows when there are spare energies and resources to invest.

At times of stress, however, attention comes again, in response to negative evaluations of the readiness of youth to protect the future. If one generation is threatened, then the next must be prepared to survive. It is the natural order of life on our planet. In order to guarantee the survival of the species, a plant compromised by drought or disease will often use its diminishing energy to produce the best blooms just before it dies. Responding to critics of the move to national testing, in his opening remarks to the summit conference, Chairman Gerstner (2001) said, "But if you listen closely, what you hear is a pathetic willingness to sacrifice an entire generation, and deny them their shot at a better chance, a better future, and a better life" (p. 2). I am sure he was also concerned about future generations.

Philosophers Durkheim (1956/1973) and Dewey (1916/1973, p. 24) remind us of the culture-preserving tasks of education. Durkheim speaks of the need for transmission of culture, but in Dewey's frame of reference, the culture must be renewed in the process of education. Dewey thus leaves the door more open to change with each new generation. And in times of stress, it is change, not continuity of anachronistic systems, that may offer the best chance for survival. Stress within our culture has increased with the quickening pace of change resulting from globalization and new technology. We will need constant renewal. As I write these words, this country is suddenly in a state of turmoil over terrorist attacks. My frame of reference today is different from the one in which I wrote last week. I will need to put my thoughts into a new historical context.

Popkewitz (2000), commenting on school reform that is based on research and evaluation using existing "commonsense" schooling as a frame of reference, states that this "denies change in the process of change" (p. 18). He envisions the political use of power in controlling education as social administration—an attempt to control chance happenings and their risks:

> The state was expected to shape a particular type of individual. . . . Policy was to police not only institutional development but also the construction of the "self" who could function within the new political relations of liberal democracy and capitalism. (p. 19)

An extreme example of nondemocratic social administration would be the unidirectional and unbending training of Hitler's youth in Nazi Germany—and, in deadly but far-reaching microcosm, the preparation for determined self-destruction of Osama bin Laden's terrorists. In contrast, cultural-transmission functions within our liberal democracy have traditionally included flexibility and responsiveness to the need for change. For most of our country's history, there has been freedom to adapt and experiment. Control of education in the United States is delegated by the Constitution to individual states, and many states have, in the past, delegated this power to local governments.

One explicatory theory in relation to this holds that when central governments lack power—in the form of desired resources (e.g., federal funds) or effective constraints—the central government introduces policies that increase deployable sanctions (Firestone, Fitz, & Broadfoot, 1999). Federal funding for education is minimal and, in the light of recent events that place us on a war status, not likely to be forthcoming. The new federal legislation, therefore, calls upon states to develop the tests and apply the sanction of forced reorganization to schools that do not meet the standards.

Dispersal of power, however, also allows for the voice of subcultures. At the same time that politicians are calling for tightening toward a traditional curriculum based on standards and assessments, albeit with the responsibility deployed to the states, are they forcing us to leave our tradition of freedom to adapt? Will greater conformity be helpful to our country?

WHAT EARLY 20TH-CENTURY SCHOOLS WERE LIKE

Schools in the early 20th century were not very different from those of the previous century. The instructional concepts and procedures of a one-room rural schoolhouse were transported to urban conglomerates of classrooms where teachers functioned more or less in isolation from each other (Lortie, 1975). The age of required attendance was extended, and consolidated high schools began to offer a wider choice of subjects for students. Most children still left before high school completion to work on family farms or in the expanding factories of the cities. Except for the greater abundance of textbooks, new technology had made little difference in either the curriculum or instructional approaches. Teachers were still trained in specialized teacher-training schools rather than in universities and were mostly female. There were some experiments in response to the ideas of progressivist philosophers such as Dewey and Froebel, but their overall influence was limited and cyclic.

In 1906, Dewey follower Samuel Wirt brought a progressive education system to the city of Gary, Indiana. His system, called the Platoon School, revolved around a combination of study, play, and work. An attempt to bring the system to New York City in 1911 was perceived as an attempt to degrade education from an intellectual enterprise to preparation for work. It actually caused some riots and turned the tide of a mayoral election (Salomon, 2001).

Resurgent infusions of variants of the concepts of progressivism, throughout the 20th century, were heralded and welcomed by educators but were then quickly dispensed with when politicians, eager to find a public interest issue, disparaged the experiments in favor of traditional methods.

MY SCHOOL IN BETHEL

My own history of involvement in educational systems in the United States has been long, varied, and challenged by change. In the beginning, at the height of the 1930s depression, there was the one-room, rural schoolhouse in Bethel, New York (also the site of the original Woodstock), which I attended while living on my grandparents' farm. The school day began with a rope-pulled bell (the student-ringer enjoying a reward for work well done), the Pledge of Allegiance, a short piece from the Bible, and the singing of the unofficial, second-place national anthem of the time, "My Country 'Tis of Thee." We then discussed the date and the weather, and Mrs. Mann shared the headlines and excerpts from the previous day's newspaper with us. This was greatly appreciated because most of us did not have regular access to newspapers, and radio reception was erratic. The morning assignments, already written on the large blackboard, were reviewed, and quickly we divided into smaller groups at two long tables or remained at our desks. The desks and chairs were movable, and every afternoon, the ink monitor would fill the individual inkwells in the desk corners. A good part of the day was spent reading aloud from our readers to Mrs. Mann or to one of the older kids. On the blackboard were math examples and spelling words to copy and use in sentences. They were organized by grade level, but we were challenged to try the harder ones. During the week, we did these on our own slates or in copybooks. Friday was test day, and the work was done on carefully counted and doled-out papers. The lined papers were folded into columns for spelling, and the unlined papers into boxes for math. Tests were returned on Monday, and we had to make the necessary corrections. We could ask Mrs. Mann or the older kids for help.

There were some textbooks that we only used in school. The textbooks were a signal for what grade we were in, but Mrs. Mann did not hesitate to move us into another grade and book at any time during the school year. I really do not remember any homework. The chores we had to do when we got home were more important. My favorite place in the schoolhouse was a little alcove with shelves of storybooks. We could read these when we finished our work, and we could take the older ones home overnight. Our school outhouse had been updated with two indoor toilets. The overhead flush tanks were filled by strokes on a lift pump, which also supplied us with drinking water. Another monitor stroked the pump regularly.

ELEMENTARY SCHOOLS
IN DEPRESSION-ERA NEW YORK CITY

My rural experiences soon alternated with some very different classrooms in depression-bound New York, where my parents migrated to try to earn a living. We had very large classes of over 40 students in the same grade and sat in long rows of attached seats. The first school I attended had been built in the middle of the 19th century. There were large supporting columns in every classroom. Punishment sometimes included sitting behind a column. The toilets we visited at morning and afternoon recess were in a separate building with girls on one side and boys on the other. They were just one long wooden bench with holes in it, but water did run through.

Every morning, we lined up for inspection. The teacher greeted us and checked us individually to see that we looked healthy, had brushed our teeth, and had brought a handkerchief. She used a pencil with an eraser on the end to look at our hair to see if there were lice. Almost everyone had free lunch, and it was welcomed. There were more textbooks, and we sometimes brought one of them home for homework. The school year was divided into two parts, A and B. Students were promoted or left back at the end of January or in June. They could also skip grades. Our classroom elementary teachers taught us everything: reading, spelling, grammar, arithmetic, history, geography, music, art, and sewing. I do not remember writing anything longer than a paragraph with our spelling words. Discipline was enforced with punishments of writing sentences about our misdeeds or, sometimes, with a smack on the palm with a wooden ruler. The schools I attended were somewhat integrated. For a short interval, I attended a school where I was a minority white student and then transferred to one where African Americans were a small minority.

In stark contrast, I had a short sojourn in the Speyer School, a Deweyan experiment in progressive education, where pursuing our own interests and understanding the world around us were supreme. We went on trips to the opera, theater, and museums; had interesting and frequent visitors; and wrote and painted pictures about what we learned. Our teachers were professors and graduate students from nearby Columbia University. I remember being impressed with how smart they were and how smart they made us feel. Best of all, I discovered, to my great surprise, that learning in school, like learning on the farm or in the store, could also be fun.

Unfortunately, I was soon back in the regular school and often bored. I never had the right place when we read aloud, because I was always thinking about what I had just read or reading ahead. The sixth grade was an exception. Mr. Nunan liked to give us all kinds of problems to solve. I remember one in particular, for which I was the only one to find a solution. A farmer had some trouble. He had a store of oil that the rats kept eating. One day, he put the oil in a bottle (for which he had no cover) and hung it from the barn rafter. The next morning, the bottle was empty, and there were no oil stains on the floor. How did the rats get at the oil? I suggested correctly that they walked along the rafter, dipped their tails into the oil, and lapped it up. I'll come back to this indirect approach in Chapter 2.

My high school was a brand-new building with the same large classes. Nevertheless, I was tracked into honors classes with some excellent teachers and less bored. We followed the prescribed New York State Regents curriculum, but I never felt that the class work was just preparation for the test. The Regents exams were combinations of short-answer, objective questions and essays; mathematics or science problems that required us to show our work; and, for foreign language, written translations. It was wartime, and education was the last thing on the public mind. Besides, going to school was a privilege to be enjoyed before going to work or war, and we all believed we were getting the very best. Success in school was entirely up to the student. My social studies teacher did adjust his curriculum to help us understand what was going on in the world. Significant history was happening every day, and our texts and what was traditionally on the Regents exam seemed less important. But he also taught us how to write a winning essay answer. Most of my homework was done between customers while sitting on a box behind the counter of my father's store, to which I traveled by city subway each day when school was finished.

I graduated before I was 16 and took the subway each day to a city college where the tuition was free. Books and bursar's fee were eight dollars a semester. My father's business had failed, and so I had all kinds of part- and full-time jobs to pay my own expenses and help somewhat with the family budget. For a while, I had to leave college and work full-time so that there would be food on the table, but I continued my chemistry and biology majors in evening classes. With any further education unaffordable, I decided, as did so many other young women with whom I communicated, that teaching was the best choice.

EDUCATION BEYOND THE CLASSROOM

> Schools are indeed one important method of the transmission [of society] which forms the disposition of the immature: but it is only one means, and compared with other agencies, a relatively superficial means. Only as we have grasped the necessity of more fundamental and persistent modes of tuition can we make sure of placing the scholastic methods in their true context. (Dewey, 1916/1973, p. 24)

I think I had a good education and certainly respected what I had learned, but in retrospect, I learned much more outside school. Living on a farm gave me the opportunity for the real-life, hands-on experiences we try to simulate for urban students today. Every day, there was a different problem to solve: flooded field or cellar, drying wells and crops, sick animals giving less milk, a new calf to be born, chicken coops needing cleaning, snow to be cleared so that we could get to the barn. Everything was constantly measured: the height of the corn, the amount of milk from a cow and the total pails for the dairy pickup, the rows of beans, the acreage in a field, the amount of flour for the bread, the best temperature of the milk for butter or cheese, the time of sunrise and sunset (and the time between), the height of the water in the kitchen well, the height of the latest snowfall, and the bushels of apples from the best tree and the volume of cider it would make. I also wandered on my own and saw nature at work. No one had to tell me about the birds and the bees—I just watched. My sense of direction developed as I watched for familiar landmarks and the position of the sun. Most important, even at a young age, I shared in the problems and solutions, was assigned to care for specific animals, and absorbed the responsibilities.

My later city life was equally instructive. In my father's grocery store, the mathematics lessons included estimating the volume of a half-pound of butter cut with a knife from a tub or comparing the volume of a pound of sugar and a pound of flour, which we weighed out carefully from larger sacks. Estimations of how many pounds were left in the sack were also important. I added a column of figures on the grocery bag faster than anyone except my mother, who taught me her making-tens addition tricks. My dad taught me the making-change tricks and trusted me at the register while I still had to stand on a box to reach it. The biology and human society lessons continued as I opened and cleaned the whole chickens we sold on weekends, hand-candled the eggs to make sure they weren't fertilized or blood spotted, and turned the fan on them to keep them fresh. I questioned why we sold so much dog food at a nickel a can—there weren't that many dogs around—and discovered it was a cheap protein meal for poor and hungry customers.

Again, the problem solving was constant. How many loaves of bread should we stock for the weekend? How should we arrange the cans on the shelves so that they could be accessed in relation to the demand for them and also make the best use of limited space? How can we gently ask a faithful customer to pay an ever-growing credit bill? Do we have enough to pay our own creditors? Our only refrigeration was a 6-foot icebox and a very small electric case. In the heat of summer, we constantly took temperatures, watched the ice in the icebox melt, and juggled perishable items.

When, on occasion, I was relieved of responsibility for my younger siblings or for helping in my parents' business, I explored the urban wonders on my own, gazing in awe at art and geological history in museums that were a nickel ride away; observing commerce on the waterfront and the social implications of race, poverty, and alcohol abuse on street corners. My favorite place and source of knowledge, however, was the public library. My library card was worn thin before it expired, as I devoured whatever I could.

The outside of school experience of children today is quite different. Greater proportions of urban living and technology have diminished many of the hands-on experiences that framed my culture. There is little opportunity to work side by side with adults as I did on the farm and in the store. However, there are still problems to solve. Some of them are, perhaps, more exigent than those I faced. There are many more resources for independent learning to choose from and greater disparity in terms of their availability for different subcultures of students. Some resources may not be good choices, and adults are not always around to offer guidance. The culture has changed. Have our expectations for schools?

SCHOOLS IN THE LATER 20TH CENTURY: A BEGINNING TEACHER

I thought about my own experiences when challenged with my first teaching assignment, an eighth-grade adjustment class in the East Harlem ghetto. I had just turned 20 and was actually recognized in a publication as one of the youngest regularly appointed teachers in the New York City schools. There was no special education in those days. Classes were, however, homogeneously grouped according to previous grades earned by the students. There were 13 regular eighth-grade classes arranged in order of ability and then three adjustment classes. There was no prescribed curriculum—at least I wasn't given one. My only instruction from the principal was to keep my door locked and the students inside the classroom until the bell rang at the end of the 40-minute period. Because they were adjustment students, they stayed with me for at least two periods at a time. I was supposed to teach them math, science, and English. They went to another teacher for social studies and, twice a week, for physical education, art, and music. When they were away, I taught other students science.

It is often recognized that in spite of current educational trends, teachers usually teach the way they were taught. Fortunately, my memories of the Speyer School and outside-of-school learning experiences dominated, and were reinforced by, the Deweyan philosophy that prevailed in my education courses. I had a clear vision of what I wanted to do. My training in science encouraged me to experiment. Free from curriculum prescriptions and untethered by the specter of imposed tests, I knew I had to make my students want to learn. And I believed, as did Dewey (1940), that interest leads to "inner motivation" and discipline (p. 155). I began to search their interests for ways to motivate these previously unsuccessful learners. We had few textbooks, and so we began to construct our own out of the picture-filled movie magazines I noticed interested many students. Our books became pasteups of cutout pictures, pieces of accompanying printed text, and the students' own written additions of personal experience and commentary. They read these to each other and vied to inject detail and humor.

Trips outside school were discouraged and almost impossible because of the schedule. I had no science laboratory in which my students could experience some of the things I had. I brought in household items and bags of specimens from nearby Central Park or the corner grocer. The nearest water was two floors below my fifth-floor classroom, but I soon had some interested students and trusted monitors to help bring it up.

Somehow, my success as a science teacher led me to an opening as an elementary science specialist in a brand-new school with a special classroom. It was actually half a greenhouse with sinks and flats for plants and room for cages. I was in teacher heaven. This was now the early 1950s—before Sputnik, copy machines, 10-pound texts, and abundant workbooks. The country was too busy with another traditional war in Korea and the cold war with Russia to pay too much attention to the education of a giant baby-boom generation. Although we had to have weekly dive-under-the-desk atomic bomb drills, the educators were in charge.

The "project method" that grew out of Dewey's focus on experience was still in the limelight, and I was encouraged to pursue it. We grew plants and boarded animals. We learned about interdependence when the rabbits ate our crops one day because someone forgot to close the cage door properly. The sex education lesson was easy when two of our box turtles remained locked in copulating position for hours at a time. Ideas about adaptation and evolution emerged when an elusive, escape artist garden snake slept the night in my clothes closet, then greeted me in the morning before bounding across the classroom, to the delight of my students.

We were encouraged to do developmental math. I loved it. We solved real problems, had bead frames and lima beans to compute with, and used thinking flash cards. Best of all, we constantly estimated and did mental arithmetic. We studied Greece, read Greek poetry and wrote some of our own, ate Greek food, and learned what Aristotle thought. There were standardized tests in math and reading at the end of the year, but there were no special preparatory exercises, admonitions, or anxiety. I knew my students were capable and was not concerned. They proved me right.

IQ TESTS AND REGENTS EXAMS

The critical assessment tool at the time was the intelligence quotient (IQ) test. With some yearly adjustment for unexpected performance, classes were basically homogeneously organized according to results of whole-group administrations of distally (i.e., away from those tested) produced versions of the Stanford revisions by Lewis Terman (Webb, Metha, & Jordan, 1996). These were usually applied in the first grade, when they were supposedly the most valid or unaffected by schooling. The IQ test compared the measured "mental age" of the child with the chronological age. The norm or standard for mental age was determined by comparing performances on the test by sample groups, and it was supposed to measure the child's inborn ability to solve "novel" problems.

The fallacy in the "objectivity" of the test was the assumption that the test items were equally novel to each child, regardless of 6 previous years of variations in the learning experience and environment. The present consensus concerning intelligence is a compromise that accepts the presence of some innate psychological or physiological components but also recognizes the powerful influences of the environment. Current debate focuses more on the various typologies, such as Gardner's (1993), which propose multiple subsets of the construct of intelligence, and on the hierarchy of skill levels and their developmental sequence.

Essentially, a student was quickly labeled with a defined potential and set of teacher expectations. At the beginning of each year, most teachers carefully listed the students in IQ order, to get some perspective of the nature of the class. There were also standardized achievement tests at the end of the school year but little attempt to connect these to our curriculum, and only minor connections of our students' performance on these tests to our own measures. With a few exceptions and minor rotations, the most experienced or promising teachers were rewarded with the top classes. Class sizes were somewhat modified downward for the "bottom" classes. The top classes ranged around 40 students and the bottom ones around 25.

My passion for science and need for personal growth eventually brought me to another New York City position at the high school level where I taught biology, chemistry, and earth science. During my first year, I was required to spend every preparation period observing an experienced teacher. At first, I resented this but soon appreciated the opportunity to learn. There was much less focus on the student's IQ at this level although it was on student records and occasionally was of interest as we compared it to the student's performance on the more dominant distal measure, the New York State Regents exam. I distinctly remember what we did after each Regents exam. All the teachers of the subject met in one room and graded and checked each other's papers. For the essay sections, there were intensive discussions about what would be considered a correct answer. As a beginning high school teacher, I learned so much about teaching and the curriculum content from these discussions with experienced colleagues.

The results on the exam were important to us. They provided affirmation that we were doing the right thing and guidance about what we needed to do better. Even as a proven, successful, tenured teacher, I couldn't wait to see how my students had performed. Although we sometimes questioned the items, we felt a comfortable sense of ownership. There was a state curriculum guide, developed with teacher input, that provided an outline we were supposed to follow, but we never felt pressured to teach in a certain way or exclude important additions. Some of us had also been involved at the state level in writing the questions, and sometimes we would call the state education department to protest or clarify a particular question. There was some opportunity for choice on the exam, and when we occasionally omitted a topic, our students were then directed to avoid the question on that topic.

DEFINING AND DEALING WITH DIFFERENCES

There were many minor cycles of school change in the early years, but all were internal to the educational establishment. There was little outside public interest. Sputnik added the first unusual external impetus for science education and an end to Dewey's progressive education. Public interest grew in the 1960s with the civil rights era, busing and integration issues raised by

President Kennedy, and the "great society" of President Johnson. The school in which I worked was already, as a whole, well integrated, but with differentiation of most classes into honors, Regents, and non-Regents levels. Although even the honors classes had some racial and ethnic variation, there were obvious socioeconomic imbalances. As a classroom teacher and then as a guidance counselor responsible for class placement, I fought to raise my own and students' expectations. But on more than one occasion, I found it difficult to convince a student, parent, or teacher colleague to stick with a more challenging class. Even more discouraging was urging a student to stay in school when the choice of staying in school—a school policy—also required giving up custody of her own child.

WHAT THE RESEARCH TOLD US

Ornstein (1975) cites conflicting reports in the findings of educational research. Jensen, for example, attributed the lack of minority success to genetics. Counteracting previous findings and diminishing public energies and interest in school reform was another piece of research: The 1966 Coleman report, which shared the findings of extensive, government-sponsored research, found few differences among the country's schools and determined the differences in success to be more related to socioeconomic class, home environment, and peers. Others believed differently. Jencks found genetics to be an influence, but to a lesser degree and mitigated by other factors.

In 1975, however, after reexamining data on international tests, Coleman recanted somewhat and admitted that schools and teaching variations did make a difference in science and literature but not in reading (Suter, 2000). I never believed otherwise. I was convinced that differences in educational quality were factors but that quality can come in more than one form.

PROVING MY POINT: GIVING STUDENTS CHOICES

In 1971, I began my administrative career as supervisor of a K-12 program in science and health. The country was embroiled in an unpopular war. Emulating their protesting college student brothers and sisters, our high school kids turned off education and on to alcohol and marijuana. The high school corridors reeked with the odor of grass, and the athletic field became the nightly hangout and beer bottle repository. It was a middle-income, New York, suburban school district, but only a small percentage of our students accepted the challenge of Regents-level classes. Only 40% of our students took a third year of high school math, and only 60% of that group passed the Regents exam. College board SAT scores were slipping rapidly. There had to be a solution! Maybe we could spend the school time in a better way. Could we lure students back to learning with a variety of electives and career education, which connected school to the real world?

By 1979, we had science electives in industrial chemistry, electronics (students built their own primitive computers), biochemistry, advanced biology, and aviation. Career education experience clusters combined in-school academic content with field experiences. State grant funding enabled me to set up clusters in health services, government, media, and recreation. Our students explored nursing, medicine, law, journalism, radio broadcasting, park management, and many other careers as they worked side by side with professionals (Solomon, 1980). A simultaneous focus on higher expectations worked in tandem with this more exciting, real-life content. Ninety percent of our seniors were in science courses—even though only 1 year was required. Research evidence now tells us that allowing students some control over the learning content and process increases motivation and achievement.

We had made some inroads into the drug and alcohol problem as well. With community help, I opened an in-town center where kids could hang out and socialize without snooping parents, but also without the drugs. Parents organized alcohol-free after-prom parties, and the police department brought us Project DARE (Drug and Alcohol Resistance Education). They also set us up with a youth court and allowed our students to judge minor youth offenses in a real courtroom.

BACK TO BASICS

The reaction to peace and a new focus on preparation for life in a burgeoning economy in the 1980s foreshadowed the current emphasis on standards and tolled the final demise of progressivism. Mortimer Adler's (1982) perennialist philosophy and Paideia Proposal spoke of the "great books" and "great ideas" that form the backbone of our culture. Adler and his followers, Hirsch (1996, 2001), who spoke of cultural literacy and core knowledge, and Alan Bloom, who referred to "cultural illiteracy as the crisis of our civilization" (Webb et al., 1996), led the foray that instigated a back-to-basics movement.

I was a middle-school principal at this time in the same suburban school district. As a group of educators, my administrative colleagues and I discussed their philosophy with mixed reactions. We appreciated the canons, but from our vantage point, we saw a new generation and a changing culture that needed renewal and, perhaps, new canons. Pressure from the state, however, caused us to abandon some of the highly successful alternatives that we had initiated in the 1970s. I was particularly disturbed that the wide choice of science and career education electives I had initiated as a science supervisor was abandoned. Most of the elective courses were replaced with the traditional Regents sequence. Instead of these choices for students, there were actions to shift the more rigorous Regents curriculum down to some eighth-grade classes so that more of the Regents-level courses and advanced-placement courses could be fit in at higher levels. Inevitably, tracking resulted, and overall enrollments in science courses were diminished.

Even my educated, middle school parents showed little interest in changing school curriculum. They rarely showed up for meetings at which curriculum was the topic of discussion. Some parents participated with teachers in the site-based management teams that were suggested at the time (this is discussed in a later paragraph) but rarely voiced strong opinions on the content of the school program. They were interested in the placement of their own children in the system, overall schedules, and issues of safety, but, generally, they wanted schools to be as much like the ones they had attended as possible.

In the cities, poverty, crime, drugs, and family dissolution widened the gaps in an increasingly diverse population. Greater local control was a suggested solution, and large city districts were decentralized. In some cities, such as Chicago, the consequences of this solution were so negative that local control was effectively abandoned. In New York City, repeating incidents of local school board corruption have caused the central board of education and its chancellor administrator to remain on constant guard. Complicating the issue, ongoing disputes between a series of incumbent chancellors and Mayors Guiliani and Bloomberg, who openly favor eliminating the central board, have created a highly volatile and unproductive atmosphere.

The attempt to solve the nation's education problems by the decentralization of power culminated in a strong effort to involve teachers and parents in site-based management. Individual school management teams were organized in our district. My own middle school management team brought us close together and generated increasing success and comfort for our teachers and students. The school that had been called "the zoo" was now the pride of the community. We actually sponsored a Pearl River Pride Day in which we engaged our students and adult volunteers in cleaning up the community. Nevertheless, the reluctance of those in power to relinquish it and the cautionary hesitation of teachers to accept responsibility for their own decisions hampered the effects of this movement. When my staff complained about the way extra classroom assignments were allocated, and I suggested to the management team that they could have the power to do the assignments, they refused to accept the responsibility for making the necessary decisions (see Chapter 7 and Solomon, 1995).

Teacher and administrative tenure is another target of reformers. Coming during a brief statewide hiatus for tenure, my first 8 years as an administrator were served without the prospect of tenure—it made little difference in my efforts. Strong protests by teacher organizations and a growing teacher shortage have curtailed momentum for this solution, but it periodically crops up.

SPECIAL EDUCATION

New laws and programs for the handicapped made us rethink our ideas on classroom organization, and all kinds of special classes were formed. Bilingual education was declared the solution to ever-increasing numbers of immigrant children. Too many students who didn't exactly fit in were tracked into these classes, forever labeled as nonachievers. Money and energy were also diverted from regular classes. Eventually, the original public acceptance for tracking was undercut by better-informed parents and by research. Research demonstrated little support for the benefits of deferring immersion into classes conducted in English. Inclusion seemed the way to go.

Confronted with newly integrated classes of students with varying abilities and simultaneous demands for meeting high standards, teachers were overwhelmed and exhausted. Differentiation of instruction was the solution for inclusion, but how can you meet the needs of every student and get them up to an imposed standard? Tomlinson (2000) suggests that teachers view differentiation not as an instructional strategy but as a philosophy that maximizes the capacity of every student. Differentiation, she contends, must be a refinement, not a substitute for high-quality curriculum. Her solution is to embed standards into the curriculum at a reasonable pace.

Technological improvements and widened access to information were heralded as major potential influences on how learning should or could happen. Films and video were followed by computers. The mimeo machine was replaced by the photocopier, and teachers and children jockeyed paper worksheets by the dozens. The final outcomes of adding computers to the classroom are still to be determined. We will address some of the possibilities for differentiation and the promise of computer technology as a possible solution to our problems in education in the chapters ahead.

Most internal efforts to transform schools in the past have been narrowly directed at specific programs, instructional strategies, or organization of the school. Sarason (1990) blamed this on the complex and intractable nature of schools and the traditional and bureaucratic power relationships within them. He accurately predicted the failure of reform that hinges only on a change in school management, the major push for teacher and parent involvement in the 1990s. In 1993, he suggested that the only possibility for true reform is to change the preparation of teachers (Sarason, 1993). Sarason did not predict the sudden emergence of the current level of political interest in education—nor did I. Never in my personal history as student and teacher has education received so much attention and external prescription for reform.

USING HISTORY AS A DECISION BASE

History is only useful in the present decision- or problem-solving process if one reflects on it in the context of the changed elements of a new time and place. For much of the previous century, curriculum and the assessment of curriculum were nominally in the power of the individual school and classroom teacher. Repeating cycles of change alternated between a focus on the developing individual and the need to perpetuate a uniform culture. A very powerful distal standard measure, the IQ test, framed major educational decisions about individual students, teachers, and groups of learners throughout most of the century's cycles. Other distally and commercially produced standardized achievement tests were based on normed samples of students and provided some overall program-evaluating benchmarks. Each of these, however, also became an instrument for sorting and labeling students, with little attention to using it to inform instruction for individuals or as a guide for reconstructing school curriculum. Less distal (proximal would be the schools' own tests) statewide standards of curriculum and articulated assessments were comfortably accepted in states such as New York and California. A long history of implementation of these tests, and time and effort to generate local ownership, made them an integral part of the school culture.

2 Schools at the Beginning of the 21st Century: Problems and Proposed Solutions

ABOUT THIS CHAPTER

This chapter brings us from the broader purview of history to the nature of the current setting. This perspective provides the bridge builder with a closer look at the specific construction problems and supports a decision-making process in which possible solutions are evaluated. Polya (1945/1956), a mathematician who examined problem-solving strategies, describes the process of induction. He tells us that in examining conjectures, the naturalist "may also reexamine the facts whose observations has led him to this conjecture, he compares them carefully, he tries to disentangle some deeper regularity, some further analogy" (p. 1980). As possible solutions are evaluated, therefore, the criteria for decision making need to hearken back to the experiences of history as well as look forward to prospective views of future hurdles and advantages.

We limit the analysis of solutions in this chapter to those that have already been proposed and tried. As we disentangle our observations, perhaps we, too, will uncover some indications of regularity and possible adaptations that might be employed in the solutions we will propose in detail in the chapters that follow.

DEFINING THE PROBLEM

The recent movement in the United States toward improving educational standards is an attempt to close the gaps among an increasingly diverse population within our own borders and in the larger world community with whom we interact. Stimulated by increasing global economic competition and burgeoning technology, the movement was formally initiated at the federal level by the *A Nation at Risk* report (National Commission on Excellence in Education, 1983). The report clearly connects education and the transmission of a changing culture to fullness of function in society:

> Learning is the indispensable investment required for success in the "information age" we are entering. . . . The people of the United States need to know that individuals in our society who do not possess the levels of literacy and training essential to this new era will be effectively disenfranchised, not simply from the material rewards that accompany competent performance, but also from the chance to participate fully in our national life. (p. 7)

This was followed by another national call for change—perhaps because of the failure of grassroots efforts to reform education and continuing reports of declining student achievement. In 1989, the National Governors Association held a national summit on education and outlined a major role for the states in educational reform—with a special emphasis on the creation of standards.

A little over a year later, Education Secretary Lamar Alexander and President George Bush announced *America 2000: An Education Strategy*, which proposed national education goals and reform strategy (U.S. Department of Education, 1991). The introduction to the announcement referred to *A Nation at Risk* and noted that "We haven't turned things around in education. Almost all our education trend lines are flat. Our country is idling its engines, not knowing enough nor being able to do enough to make America all that it should be." The president suggested that the goals would allow states to gauge whether students are meeting "national standards of excellence" in those subjects. Hopefully, he added that, "This emphasis on testing national standards will not incite the struggle to define the role of the federal and state governments in education" (p. 9).

Goal 3 of the National Goals (U.S. Department of Education, 1991) states that "The academic performance of all students at the elementary and secondary levels will increase significantly in every quartile, and the distribution of minority students in each quartile will more closely reflect the student population as a whole" (p. 3). Apparently, the goals have not all been met. The nation's performance on the National Assessment of Educational Progress (NAEP), our own test, that has been given in the past to a controlled sample of volunteer schools to assess the progress of our nation's schools in reading and in mathematics, has shown only minimal improvements.

At first glance, the overall numbers of students reaching standard levels seem optimistic on the most recent NAEP tests. However, careful analysis comparing the top and bottom quartile of students shows a widening gap between them and "little progress in closing the white/minority achievement gap" (Barton, 2001, p. 11). Although fourth- and eighth-grade average math scores have improved significantly in participating states, fourth- and eighth-grade reading scores, and the difference between the bottom and top quartile scores on the eighth-grade math test, are a continuing problem. Most disappointing was the news that between 1992 and 1998, only one state reduced the reading gap.

To add fuel to the fire, the 1992 performance by U.S. students on the math portion of the Third International Math and Science Study (TIMSS), an international and worldwide comparison that includes 25 industrialized and developing countries, had been disappointing. A repetition of the TIMSS study in 1999 showed some improvement at the lower grades, but the country still lagged behind its industrialized counterparts at the upper grade levels (Mullis et al., 2000). Perhaps our returning astronaut (see Chapter 1) should speak to former astronaut and senator John Glenn. Glenn headed a commission appointed by Secretary of Education James Riley. Glenn's report, "Before It's Too Late" (National Commission on Mathematics and Science Teaching, 2000), underscored the poor performance of the nation's students on these tests. The report listed four reasons that students needed to be competent in math and science: the interdependent global economy; the need for math and science in everyday decision making; national security interests; and the value of knowledge in our common life, history, and culture.

Although the report focused on math and science, these four reasons transfer easily to other subjects and define the reasons for the federal government's concern. Lack of appreciable progress in mitigating this concern is neither unexpected nor due to failure on the part of educators and local governments to make attempts to improve schools. It is the problem at hand. Changing schools, as I have indicated in Chapter 1 and previous books, is not an easy feat. It takes time and carefully evaluated experiments to find the appropriate solutions. A thoughtful examination of history and setting requires us to look at solutions previously suggested before deciding on our own.

PROPOSED SOLUTION ONE: DEFINING EDUCATIONAL STANDARDS

Although the test results seem valid, the recommendations for ameliorating the problem are grounded in several, as yet unproven, assumptions and beliefs about education in the United States. These include the belief that clearly stated and uniform standards and technologically rich instruction will alone result in higher student achievement in this country when it is compared to student achievement on an international basis, as well as the belief that high-stakes measures will guarantee the implementation of the standards (McCaslin, 1996; Natriello, 1996).

As they have already been developed by states and professional organizations such as the National Council of Teachers of Mathematics (NCTM) and the New Standards Program (a coalition of the Learning and Research Development Center and the National Center on Education and the Economy), standards are essentially outcomes or receiver-based objectives. They retain the design-down potential of outcome-based instruction but differ in their intent from goals and objectives in that they are prescriptions designed for the purposes of higher expectations and uniformity.

The use of the term *standards* instead of the traditional educator's term *objectives* foreshadowed a strengthening of government's determination and role in social administration. Both terms essentially entail a process of coming to consensus and explicit statements of the elements of the American culture worthy of transmission. In this respect, the standards parallel traditional goals and objectives as well as outcomes. The term *standard*, however, has an implication of high levels of expectation and monitoring that were not commonly connected to the widely used educational objectives suggested by Tyler (1949) as clarified statements of school curriculum. Although both the consensus of what students should know and be able to do and the measures of how well they know and are able to do are included in standards documents—most often as separate content standards and performance standards—the greatest emphasis has been on the performance measures. It is the monitoring process on national and international levels that has energized the rising concerns systems.

Interestingly, the first formal presentation of national standards came as an indirect message from a group of educators with little nominal power and no ability to apply sanctions. When the NCTM (1989) published its standards, they were very well received by almost everyone concerned. Mathematics is a subject that is probably the least culturally controversial. School districts did major curriculum work and staff development, and new commercial textbook programs were developed. Contrary to present conceptions of standards, the NCTM proposals did not hearken back to a rosy past.

Instead, they focused on the new curriculum needed in an increasingly technological future, and incorporated the instructional guidelines suggested by what researchers were discovering as most effective.

There was some backlash from parents who did not understand the changed focus on constructivism. The goal of the constructivist approach is to build greater understanding and ability to apply mathematical processes. It involves increased emphasis on problem solving, mental arithmetic, estimation, and use of manipulatives—and less emphasis on algorithms (National Council of Teachers of Mathematics, 1989). Parents were sometimes not educated to the ultimate value of this approach and protested about the missing content they remembered in the worksheets and algorithm drills that they had experienced as students. Teachers, who were often inadequately prepared, also were uncomfortable with teaching and thinking in a way that they themselves had not experienced as students.

In some places, impatience with the changes was intensified by reports of poor performance on tests. There is always a lag with innovations in education, and the tests themselves may need to be adjusted. The backlash and political pressure, however, were enough to cause even NCTM to put a greater emphasis on content in its year 2000 revision of the standards. My own successful experience with implementing constructivist math is documented in a previous book, *No Small Feat* (Solomon, 1995). I will discuss in greater detail in Chapter 4 some of the factors that contributed to the success of this endeavor.

Other professional organizations followed suit, but none of the standards statements were quite as successfully disseminated by the organizations themselves. Following the *America 2000* announcement, however, many state and local efforts to set standards have been based on the work of the professional organizations. Perhaps the coldest reception and reactive furor followed the publication of the *Curriculum Standards for Social Studies: Expectations of Excellence by the National Council for the Social Studies (NCSS)* (1994). These were certainly not value or issue free. New York State Commissioner of Education Richard Mills explained his preference for traditional subject area organization thusly:

> You can easily get lost in this, and it has caused some people to get very touchy-feely-fuzzy about what they expect. And that has opened the standards movement to charges from more conservative folks who worry about government and school intruding into issues of values. (Lehman & Spring, 1996, p. 8)

In its attempt to be politically correct, the NCSS document precipitated the first vehement protest against standards. The subject of social studies is the one most vulnerable to the needs and influences of subcultures. Resistance to integration into a single culture should have been expected.

In spite of the furor created by some of the social studies inclusions and lack of them, several states still used much of the NCSS work in developing their own standards but carefully explained that new inclusions did not exclude other important items. The states have assumed a major role in the curriculum standards endeavor. With the exception of Iowa, every state now has sets of standards and assessments. We need to give the state standards more time: time for building shared communicative consensus among teachers, administrators, and parents; time to make the needed changes in teachers' skills and materials; and time to make the appropriate matches between the standards and our measures of their accomplishment.

PROPOSED SOLUTION TWO: SCHOOL ACCOUNTABILITY

The continued lackluster performance of students on the national and international tests has suddenly become a major political issue. Education is a relatively safe issue for politicians—everyone is for better schools. It was a major agenda issue for President Clinton and near the top of the list in the presidential campaign. With the new administration of President George W. Bush in January 2001, the focus of attention moved quickly from curriculum standards, which offered a needed consensus of the cultural constructs worthy of transmission, to school accountability. Accountability implies the use of measures and sanctions. Holding schools accountable for what they do by taking measures with mandated testing could be part of the solution to our present crisis—if the testing is appropriately applied. Assessment has always been a part of our school culture. As an individual teacher and administrator, I welcomed the opportunity for some outside checkpoint—it gave me comfort and validity. Mandated measures can work to improve instruction if they are valid, match the curriculum, and generate appropriate responses. The responses must include change, not just in the systems of instructional delivery, the skills of the teachers, and the performance of the students, but, at times, in the substance of the tests themselves. And time is needed for change.

Over time—going back to Dewey's concept of educational experience as renewal—assessments must also be responsive to changes in society and to variations in the curriculum. In periods of stress, solutions may be found in the variations. Again, from my biologist's perspective, in Darwin's explication of how we humans got to be as good as we are at surviving, it is random chance that brings about the best opportunities. Even one adventitious mutation can sometimes make the difference.

THE GOVERNMENT RESPONSE: HIGH-STAKES TESTING

Instead of offering the flexibility of innovative solutions to diagnosed problems in a changing culture, the recommended remedy of government is tighter control and high-stakes testing. Any formal evaluation that has appreciable consequences for an individual, school, or system is considered high stakes. An example of tight control is the persistence of the New York State Commissioner of Education Richard Mills in not allowing teacher- and parent-supported alternatives to the Regents tests—some quite demanding and successful—as a requirement for graduation. In protest, parents from the affluent district of Scarsdale, New York, boycotted eighth-grade exams by keeping their children home on test day, and accompanied their high school student picketers for the 150-mile journey to the state capital of Albany with signs that read, "I am not a test score." The commissioner initiated an investigation of the source of the protest, and a legal suit by parents is also in process (Bert, 2001; Hartocollis, 2001).

Rod Paige, secretary of education, however, maintained the significance of tests with his remark that:

> When states commit to using assessment data—and by this I mean breaking down results and holding schools accountable for the performance of all of their students—they see real improvement in student achievement. President Bush and Congress can lay the groundwork for reform, but state standards and assessments are the real mechanisms for improving student achievement. (U.S. Department of Education, 2001)

Accountability also implies sanctions for school failure or lack of progress. This makes the assessment high stakes. The most recent sanctions proposed have moved up from the embarrassment of press releases, which compare school-to-school performance, to state takeovers or required reorganization and changes in management, and, finally, to the withholding of federal funds.

The final law (No Child Left Behind Act of 2001) signed on January 8, 2002, by President George W. Bush, responds to his campaign promise that "No child shall be left behind." It calls for mandated testing every year in Grades 3 to 8, to be implemented by the school year 2005 to 2006, and a set of consequences should schools not meet the requirement of value-added progress (comparing scores from year to year). The bill was a compromise that gave parents the right to change schools within the district if the mandate was not met, and lack of progress over a 3- to 5-year period would mandate several actions including the following:

- If a school fails to make progress for 2 consecutive years, it will be identified as needing improvement and must develop improvement plans incorporating strategies from scientifically based research.
- School districts will be required to offer public school choice (unless prohibited by state law) to all students in the failing school no later than the first day of the school year following identification. The district must provide transportation to the new school.
- If a school fails to make progress for a third consecutive year, the district must continue to offer public school choice and provide Title I funds (approximately $500 to $1,000 per child) for low-achieving, disadvantaged students in the school to obtain supplemental services—tutoring, after-school services, or summer school programs—from the public- or private-sector provider selected by their parents from a state-approved list.
- Twenty percent of Title I funds at the local school district level must be used for public school choice and supplemental services.
- If a school fails to make progress for a fourth consecutive year, it will be subject to increasingly tough corrective actions—such as replacing school staff or significantly decreasing management authority at the school level. If a school continues to fail, the school could ultimately face restructuring, which involves a fundamental change in governance, such as a state takeover or placement under private management.

Accompanying the sanctions, however, were the additional funds described in Chapter 1 and greater flexibility in how the funds were spent.

HIGH-STAKES TESTING:
THE OTHER STAKEHOLDERS RESPOND

When the emphasis on reform moves from clarification of curriculum, now in the form of content standards with some leeway for local adaptation, to inflexible standardization and accountability measures, the reactions of educators have, in general, been negative.

After a career spent in research on educational testing, Linn (2000) comes to the unfortunate conclusion that:

In most cases the instrumentation and technology have not been up to the demands that have been placed on them by high-stakes accountability. Assessment systems that are useful monitors lose much of their dependability and credibility for that purpose when high stakes are attached to them. The unintended negative effects of the high-stakes accountability uses often outweigh the intended positive effects. (p. 14)

Linn's conclusions are based on a combination of factors including the unreliability of single tests as determinants, the historical record that demonstrates second-year improvements for new tests followed by smaller gains, if any, and the selective exclusion of some students from tests. His suggestions include examining year-to-year or value-added results, rather than making school-to-school comparisons (as implemented in the final bill described earlier in this chapter), and accounting for uncertainty in the results. Linn's further recommendation is that in order for standards to be useful, they must be more specific and must serve as a guide for the constructs measured by the tests.

On an international level, based on studies in the United Kingdom and the United States, Firestone, Fitz, and Broadfoot (1999) agree with Linn. They admit that assessment policy is useful for promoting easily observable changes and can influence what topics are taught, but they conclude that the policy is less able to influence teachers' instructional approaches. Linn's recommendation for matching constructs and specificity are possible solutions to this lack of impact on instructional practice; and it is one that we pursue in greater detail in Chapter 5.

In most cases, teachers and parents would agree. Barksdale-Ladd and Thomas (2000) report the findings of interviews with teachers and parents in two states, which searched for reactions to high-stakes tests. Among the significant results were the common feelings of stress for teachers, parents, and students created by the tests; a feeling by teachers that the tests were contradictory to everything they had learned about what was important for children; and for some, the lack of acceptance of the appropriateness of the standards on which the tests were based. Teachers judged their teaching "worse instead of better" because of test preparation, and they expressed some concern that people would be turned away from the profession. Most parents also saw little value in the tests. The lack of involvement by teachers or teacher-educators and researchers in test development by states was noted and may be a major reason for the lack of their acceptance.

When the shoe is on the other foot and tests are forced on states by federal initiative, the response is similar. Reaction in July 2001 by state school chiefs to the proposed legislation was overwhelmingly negative. Already reeling from the costs of their own newly designed tests and weathering the backlash from parents and teachers, they viewed the additional tasks and enormous cost of again redesigning their programs as undoable. They complained about the infringement on their local control and the additional focus on testing rather than on improving teaching. California superintendent Delaine Eastin expressed the common opinion that just testing is not the magic remedy. Instead, she suggested that what was needed was a powerful curriculum, time for change, and teacher training (Wilgoren, 2001). We will return to Eastin's remedies in Chapters 5, 6, and 7.

Some of the reactions to the proposed legislation were unpredictable or ambivalent. Most New York state legislators in both the senate and house voted for the federal bills in spite of the projected costs to the state and the complaints of teachers. Although the teachers have complained, their union, the New York State United Federation of Teachers, supports the legislation. As voiced by Executive Vice President Alan Lubin, "Teachers hate the tests, but it promises more federal funding for teacher training, literacy programs and education for the disadvantaged" (Wilson, 2001a). Instructed to abandon everything but preparation for the fourth-grade tests, many tenured teachers resist teaching at that grade, and the responsibility is left to those who are inexperienced and nontenured (Goodnough, 2001a).

Some state governments are slowing their timetables in response to the negative reactions. In September 2001, the Arizona Department of Education suspended the Arizona Instrument to Measure Standards (AIMS) test, giving high school students a break from the testing regimen. Arizona Department of Education officials also hired a new private testing contractor for $29 million over 5 years to retool the test and create new test questions (Flannery, 2001). We will address the scenario in Massachusetts in Chapter 3. Even President George W. Bush wavered on his original promise to measure the gaps between the high- and low-performing students. The Senate bill he favored allowed for averaging the results rather than disaggregating them by race, poverty, and ethnicity as the House bill did.

The approach in the final version of the legislation is an attempt to move away from the unfairness of school-to-school competition among schools with different populations by using value-added test analysis that examines progress over the years in a particular school. This process may also be flawed. In a study of previous yearly test scores in two well-performing states (North Carolina and Texas), Kane and Staiger (2001) discovered that using the House of Representatives criteria would cause more than three quarters of schools in those states to be restructured over the 5-year period. The Senate bill would have mandated the restructuring of one quarter of the schools. The problem with value-added test analysis is that because of normal fluctuations in students, teaching staffs, and differences in the tests themselves, test scores do not always follow a straight path. Even the temperature on the day of the test can make a difference. There are also recognizable patterns with new forms of testing, with better results the second and third times they are administered, and then a noticeable lag in progress.

For these and other reasons, educational researchers and teacher-educators are almost universally opposed to the accountability focus. In 1975, Allan Ornstein implored,

> Will the advocates of accountability be found out? Will we come to realize that it is useless and unfair to hold teachers accountable for something they have little control over? Will the people and politicians admit that we cannot deliver on most of our promises to equalize education; that each student brings to school different equipment to learn? (p. 7)

McNeil (2000) reiterated this reaction and then expanded on the consequences: "The central message is that educational standardization harms teaching and learning, and, over the long term, restratifies education by race and class" (p. xxvii).

These reactions by researchers to standardization and accountability are not unexpected. The findings of much educational research in the recent past have been that attention to differences in the home and school contexts of learning environments was vital to an understanding of the variations in performance among students. Remedies, suggested by researchers for these variations in performance, would need to consider the contextual differences as well as the very individual pyschosocial needs of students.

The public and media have similar concerns about the singularity of standards. Zernike (2001) calls it a Goldilocks syndrome: "If the standards are too high, not many children can reach them. Set them too low, they become meaningless and risk boring the smarter children" (p. B1). There is, then, a search for the just-right standard, but the expedient measure by the New York City Board of Education was to implement a second-higher track for math classes.

In my vision, clear statements of standards and expectations do not preclude the attention to student and contextual differences, as long as there is reasonable flexibility in the methods for reaching them, appropriate provision for the different needs, and alternate and reasonable measures. There is nothing wrong with the goal of being above the standard, and individual schools can set such goals. I want to know where I am going, but I want the freedom to choose my own best path.

PROPOSED SOLUTION THREE: ACHIEVING EQUITY THROUGH SCHOOL CHOICE

Following the landmark *Brown v. Topeka Board of Education* decision in 1954 and numerous other court actions in the next 3 decades, the hope for closing achievement gaps lay in desegregation of schools. Children were bused far distances to accomplish this. Unfortunately, white flight to the suburbs overcame this potential for improving schools by mixing peers and cultures. Recent research and changes in attitude have refocused attention on the possibilities of peer influence, and we will address these in Chapter 7. An immediate response to the shifting of populations, however, was to offer parents the choice to send their children away from the local district to another school. One form of choice was the magnet school concept. Magnets were specialized schools with attractions that would, hopefully, stop the population migration by eliminating the neighborhood school concept and give everyone the opportunity to attend a selected school. This developed further into the current concepts of choice and charter schools in a free market.

Apple (2001) eruditely sums up the political forces that energize the current calls for action. He sees a new alliance and power bloc of neoliberal and conservative groups "whose overall aims are providing the educational conditions necessary for increasing international competitiveness, profit and discipline and for returning us to a romanticized past of the ideal home, family and school" (pp. 183-184).

Among the solutions proposed by this power bloc, and included as sanctions in the legislation considered in 2001, is allowing parents greater choice in selecting the schools their children attend. The concept involved is that of setting up a market economy for schools so that competition between individual schools will improve them. Apple (2001) cites the failure of this approach in other countries, such as England and New Zealand, and also points out that middle-class parents are best equipped to shop the markets and "work the system." That leaves the poorer students behind in less successful schools and the performance gaps between the classes unclosed. Because of the somewhat distorted selection of students as described earlier, and the difficulty in controlling all the variables that affect student achievement, we do not, as yet, have any clear evidence that charter schools and parent choices have made much difference in the overall performance of students.

In his analysis of the achievement results of students in schools of choice, Goldhaber (1999) found that despite increased spending, student scores in much heralded programs, such as programs in the Alum Rock and Richmond schools in California, did not improve. Although magnet schools within a school district tend to have test scores above the district average, Goldhaber points out that they usually have selection criteria. The magnet schools also tend to attract students who do better on tests than students who do not make the choice.

An evaluation of the extensive school choice program in Milwaukee, Wisconsin, revealed interesting results from a comparison between students who were accepted by the private schools for which they applied or who were unaccepted and, therefore, continued in public school. Although there was little difference for the first two years, there was a measurable positive difference for accepted students in the third and fourth years. A 30% attrition rate from the private schools, however, raises the question of whether those who would have performed poorly left.

Charter schools are a hybrid between public and private education and depend on school vouchers, which subsidize student attendance. School vouchers for charter schools were among President Bush's original 2001 agenda for school improvement. Because charter schools are private, they have greater freedom to innovate and are very diverse. Detractors argue that because of the differential between the voucher sums and the actual cost for attending the schools, poorer students would be eliminated. The results of charter schools are still too new to allow us to form any firm conclusions. There are, however, lessons to be learned from a number of successful and unsuccessful experiments. One of the reasons that students in private and charter schools may do better is the influence of peers.

PROPOSED SOLUTION FOUR: EXTENDING THE TIME FOR SCHOOLING

A common solution for lack of progress in any endeavor is to try and try again. Trying takes time, and, as we shall see in Chapter 3, time is a significant variable in the process of change. Suggestions for extending the time for school-based experience include lengthening the year with summer sessions or year-round schools, after-school remedial programs, and prekindergarten education. All these choices represent major additional public investments in education. They also make assumptions about the total energy of children to learn in a traditional school environment. Given the constraints of limited funds to support extra time, and the limitations of children's learning energy, the criteria for making the appropriate or best choice must include evidence of success. After the summer school programs of 1999, it was discovered that students in at least six states, including 9,000 from New York City, had been mistakenly sent there because of errors in the commercially calculated test scores on which their placement was based. In the summer of 2001, approximately 72,000 New York City students in Grades 3 to 8 were required to attend summer school programs. Only 56% of the high school students and 76% of the elementary group assigned showed up (Goodnough, 2001c). Of these, more than half failed the program's tests. Much of the failure was probably due to lack of consistent attendance. The mind-set of parents and children is still that summer is vacation time, and human beings do need periods of rest and sometimes summer jobs to help their families. Rest, however, can come in the form of different kinds of experiences. Time for more of the same may not be the solution.

TIME FOR ENRICHMENT

For many years, I managed a math and science enrichment program for 5th- to 12th-grade students on Saturday morning. The program, Search for Solutions, was taught by teaching teams of scientists or college faculty and secondary school teachers. It exposed students to practicing scientists, often in the real-science environment of their workplace. They streaked hundreds of bacterial plates using a robot at a local drug manufacturing plant; isolated DNA; explored pollution in local streams; and used computer interface probes at an IBM facility to measure light, sound, and other variables. Enrollment in the program was voluntary and the cost mostly subsidized by a state grant. The number of students increased each year, and minority enrollment grew from only 10% to nearly 50% for the final year, when other state priorities eliminated funds. Evaluations of the program by students and their parents were overwhelmingly positive. Parents often commented that it was easier to get students ready to come on Saturday than it was to get them up for school the rest of the week.

There were no tests of content, but 8 years of evaluations indicated that the students were transferring the increased interest generated by the Saturday experiences to their regular school programs, and there was also evidence of higher enrollment in advanced courses and plans for pursuit of careers in science. We will revisit the Saturday morning Search for Solutions program in Chapters 6 and 7. The jury is still out on extending the time for schooling, but my own experience tells me that in order to be effective, the time spent must be different.

TIME FOR A GOOD START

Prekindergarten education for all children may be different. Evidence is mounting that good prekindergarten experiences, such as the Head Start programs, are effective. A longitudinal study released by the National Center for Educational Statistics (NCES) (1999) revealed that although the entering basic-skills gap between advantaged and disadvantaged children diminished in the kindergarten year, the emergent literacy-skills gap widened. A holistic review of the research on prekindergarten education by the National Research Council (NRC) (2000) attributes this difference to quality cognitive stimulation and rich language stimulation in the homes or preschool experiences of advantaged children. Recent research into early brain development and learning abilities has shown the young child to be more capable of abstractions than previously believed. The differences in these formative abstractions may create an ever-widening gap as the child progresses through school. Attendance of all children in prekindergarten programs has increased from 53% in 1991 to 60% in 1999. Attendance in center-based programs by African American children increased from 58% to 73%, but only 44% of Hispanic children attended such programs.

The conclusions of the NRC study are that the programs vary greatly; that the quality of the early experience makes a big difference; and that what we believe applies, as well, to the entire school experience. Montgomery County, Maryland's full-day kindergarten program appears to have helped students improve reading skills, according to a new, yearlong study issued by the county's school district. The study of nearly 8,000 kindergartners found that 71% of high-risk students who spent all day in school had mastered reading fundamentals by the end of the year, as opposed to 54% of those enrolled in half-day programs (Gowen, 2001).

In reflecting on this progress, however, Montgomery Superintendent of Schools Jerry Weast (Montgomery County Public Schools, 2001) attributed gains in closing the achievement gap between affluent and poverty-stricken students to a spectrum of reforms that supplemented the extra time. These included an emphasis on smaller classes in the earliest grades, a more academic curriculum, and extensive kindergarten teacher training. We will begin to address our strategies for measuring and improving quality in Chapter 4.

PROPOSED SOLUTION FIVE: TECHNOLOGY IN THE CLASSROOM

One much-heralded solution to our problems in education in the late 1990s was the increased use of technology. Many school districts made major investments in hardware and software. The first-generation software that is still in place in many schools today was little more than a replication of print materials. This first generation of computer-assisted instruction (CAI) did, however, have an advantage over print materials in its immediate-feedback and student-control components. It fed students' needs for interest, self-efficacy, and their intrinsic goals. It was that kind of motivation that produced the current generation of technology users. Although this software has been in use in schools for more than a decade, it has never really been integrated into the curriculum. Like dittos from an extra workbook, the software programs were add-ons that the kids seemed to like.

The advent of CD-ROMs, with their multimedia potential for interactive engagement of the learners, not only heightened the previous motivational advantages for students but also introduced greater variation in the stimulus and response modalities. If kids have to make choices about how to design an airship that they can then race or are placed in a simulated environment where they have to find their way out, they face a different and more constructive challenge than if they only read about airplanes. And the Internet has expanded this potential exponentially. If students can use their programs to directly access scientific databanks to help them make predictions about earthquakes or sunspots, they are beyond a level that any traditional classroom, with the best possible teacher, can provide. If they use their programs to communicate visually and individually with the scientists who collected this data, they are reaching beyond the (still necessary) human interactions of their own cooperative groups. If they use computer-interfaced environmental probes, wind tunnels, and bridge constructions to gather environmental data and make original designs, they have not only used technology as a tool to learn something that is already known by others, but they have also used it to create completely new knowledge.

THE RESEARCH BASE FOR TECHNOLOGY USE

The research literature on the use of technology in the classroom is slim, descriptive, and intuitive in terms of its impact. Windschitl (1998) reminds us that this research does not ask critical questions such as "How is the introduction of technology changing pedagogical practices?" and "Are these practices helping students, and if so, how?" (p. 28). Hill and Somers (1996) remind us that "Technological tools in the classroom lose meaning without consideration of the basic nature of the teaching-learning process" (p. 305). Woodward and Rieth (1997) point out that it soon became clear that CAI was, by itself, "insufficient as a teaching medium" (p. 515). They do report substantive findings for the role of technology in supporting some of the metacognitive (or learning goal and control) factors, which have been proven to positively affect variables in other research. For example, the immediate feedback of informal assessment is more effective in developing self-efficacy when it is task specific rather than general (Pintrich, Mark, & Boyle, 1993). Good educational technology has built in task-specific assessment components, and the feedback is immediate and private.

Although drill and practice software did little to impact the overall instructional practices, new generation software and Internet access may have a stronger impact, especially if we pay attention to what we learn from it. In addition to providing the opportunity for the assessment and feedback of CAI, the newer technology of the Web adds the perceptions and interactions that come directly from social interactions with others outside the traditional classroom and with social artifacts beyond those we formerly were limited to (Owston, 1997). It can structure the problem-solving situations and simulations that add form, interest, and meaning to the classroom stage.

Technology addresses the need to make curriculum responsive to varying learning styles and multiple intelligences (Gardner, 1993). Computers can change the way we interact with text, using sounds, images, and video to enhance understanding as we read and create documents. In cooperative-learning environments, technology can promote social exchange; it can create students who are global citizens and teachers who learn and share with their counterparts around the world.

If second graders can write their book reports and design their PowerPoint presentations so that others will want to read their books, they have reached a new level of communication skill. If social studies classes can maintain ongoing communications with students from all over the world, get original geographic and economic data from databanks in the countries they are studying, or original transcripts of congressional discussions, and then use these communications and information to simulate new situations and make decisions, they are doing something my teachers never dreamed of.

TECHNOLOGY AS AN ASSESSMENT TOOL AND MANAGER

An unrecognized advantage of educational use of technology is its privacy. If you make a mistake, no one notices except the computer, and it offers quick and plentiful opportunities for experimentation and self-correction. Technology may form lifelong habits of self-assessment and comfort with trying new ways of doing things. Greater control, choice, and privacy combine to make learning through computers intrinsically motivating.

Technology allows teachers to manage and assess the variables in their students' performance, and in their own. There are a number of excellent commercial programs that help teachers monitor individual student achievement. They can also be used to quickly disaggregate data to identify subgroup differences, particular concept areas of greatest group need, or even to identify deficient assessment items. I will address the significance of disaggregated data in Chapter 4.

One alternative approach to assessment that can incorporate technology is the portfolio. Portfolios represent a belief in the view that assessment should take into account process, product, growth, achievement, and individual difference. In their role as systematic collections and representations that serve as the basis for examining effort, improvement, processes, and achievement, portfolios fulfill the need for greater breadth in the assessment process. Valencia and Place (1994) embrace three major concepts that support portfolio assessment: alignment with curriculum, student engagement in their own learning and evaluation, and student growth over time. They state that while the impetus for portfolio assessment grew out of a desire for more authentic assessment, the importance of portfolios centers on their potential to enhance both teaching and learning. They note that portfolios encourage students to engage in self-reflection and self-evaluation and encourage teachers to critically evaluate their instruction and use portfolio information to make instructional decisions.

THE CURRENT STATUS OF THE USE OF TECHNOLOGY IN SCHOOLS

Schools were so busy with the acquisition of the technology that they did not have time to carefully assess exactly how the technology could be connected to curriculum and the learning-teaching process. Most applications were diverted to the position of curriculum additions rather than to a role as an integral part of in-school learning. Public schools in several states, including Texas and New York, have had mixed results with the introduction of computers. In Florida, a small school district has equipped each child with a specially equipped laptop computer and plans that each child will spend 2 hours of each school day using it. Nevertheless, the children prefer their own computers at home because they have games on them (Mercer, 2001).

Trotter (1998) reminds us that it has been over twenty years and billions of dollars spent since the personal computer was first used in schools, and that the public and the policymakers are beginning to demand evidence of its effectiveness. He identifies one difficulty in determining its effectiveness as a lack of consensus on its purpose. My questions of its purpose are: Can technology make teachers change the way they teach? Can technology be the solution to our achievement gap? We may have to wait a while to find out.

With the advent of the new emphasis on high-stakes, standards-based (HSSB) testing, some of the energy has been diverted from preparing schools and teachers for the applications of technology. Although technology is included in the New York state standards, it is not tested—and that does make a difference! Some of the original motivational interest of the students and their teachers has also been diminished by the presence of computers at home—students frequently surpassed their teachers in technology skills. This enhanced and broadened informal learning, but while it allowed more student control, perhaps it diverted learning energy from what was on the tests. I watch my grandchildren run to their games, search the Internet for game codes and eBay bargains, and communicate on chat rooms, while the boring homework waits until they are too tired to really care.

The unequal presence of home computers has also widened the gaps between those who do and do not have home access. A U.S. Department of Commerce study (2000) found that African American and Hispanic children are far less likely to have a computer at home than white children. According to the survey, about 77% of white children have a computer at home; 72% of Asian and Pacific Islander children do; yet only 43% of African American children and 37% of Hispanic children have a computer at home. The report also noted that given the disparity in home computer use, computer access at schools and public libraries is critical for these children.

A study by the Educational Testing Service (ETS) (1998) based on National Assessment of Educational Progress (NAEP) tests revealed that African American rural and urban students were less likely to have home computers and, when in school, were less likely to use them for higher-order tasks. The higher-order uses, such as those mentioned earlier, were linked to higher achievement on the NAEP tests (Educational Testing Service, 1998). Trying to overcome this discrepancy, a number of public schools have enlisted the help of private entrepreneurs (especially technology producers) to equip each child with a laptop computer.

Technology can enable us to do new things, otherwise impossible, in the school setting; using it can improve many traditional things we do, but understanding how it works may also teach us how to improve the many worthwhile things we can do without it.

Table 2.1 summarizes the connections between what we know from research about what works for learning, curriculum, and assessment—and the possible advantages of using technology. Included are several advantages for the assessment process. These are in indicated in boldface.

TECHNOLOGY FOR COMMUNICATING WITH OUR PUBLIC

Technology can help us do a better job of communicating with parents and the public (Owston, 1997). It can also bring us help from others. Parents with computers no longer need to ask, "What did you do today?" if they can get an online report from the teacher. Many schools and classes now have Web pages where students can post and share their work. Absent students can get assignments and interact with classmates at school. The school district in which I live has many students who come from economically deprived homes without computers. For the future, we have planned to put them in community centers and local businesses that want to help with access for the children. The libraries and churches already have them. We also envision a volunteer corps of community online homework helpers. Greater involvement by these individuals may engender greater knowledge of what we do, and greater trust in our efforts may be the unexpected result.

We will, however, have to be careful what we send home. Student report cards online may still be requested, but reading students' stories, viewing

(text continues on page 41)

Table 2.1 Learning Curriculum, Assessment, and the Technology Advantage

Theory or Finding	Inference for Curriculum and Assessment	Technology Advantage
All individuals must construct their own new reality or knowledge based on connections between previous knowledge and new experiences. Individuals construct new adaptations of knowledge as a result of actions on the environment or interactions with others.	The curriculum should provide experience-rich environments that promote opportunities for students to learn with understanding as active participants, rather than environments that rely on passive students and teacher telling.	Technology can provide a rich and active environment. It facilitates inquiry and invention, discovery and exploration of relationships and patterns, higher-order cognitive tasks such as the **critical assessment of data,** compare-and-contrast activities, and transformation of information into something new.
The construction of new knowledge is enhanced in active or *doing* situations, particularly those that present high–interest, novel situations.	Learning environments should provide for active participation in real-life situations, problem solving, and **self-assessment.**	Technology allows time for reflection.
The construction of new or ever-changing adaptations of knowledge is governed by human goals.	The curriculum should pay attention to and address student goals such as affiliation, control, interest, and efficacy.	Technology allows for control and choice. It can provide immediate, positive **assessment** feedback in small increments that impart self-efficacy.
Human goals can be interpreted in terms of the affective factors, such as motivation, self-efficacy, attitude, and interest, that have previously demonstrated and recognized effects on learning.	Students need to be interactive and in more control—even engaged in **self-assessment.** The curriculum should consider the differences in individual and cultural goals and provide an environment that enlists or modifies those goals toward the purpose of learning.	Its impersonal and private nature decreases the risk of making, admitting, and trying to correct a mistake. It changes the classroom from a teacher-centered one to a student- and activity-centered one.
The building of self-efficacy is managed by the **assessment** process.	Activities need to be realistic and interesting and to allow students to achieve at ever-more-challenging levels, without dependence on extrinsic rewards.	*Classrooms need to be student centered.*

Theory or Finding	Inference for Curriculum and Assessment	Technology Advantage
New knowledge and goals are frequently framed and modified on a social plane. New knowledge is constructed as a mediator stretches the child from previously internalized knowledge to new knowledge.	Teachers need to plan for this stretching by carefully matching environments and planned outcomes or standards. These standards are the knowledge of the *consensual domain*.	Technology increases the opportunity for the teacher to structure authentic learning environments and discovery of the standards or knowledge of the *consensual domain*.
The knowledge that children then share, and that others may share, is in the *consensual domain*. The social plane may involve social artifacts, such as texts and computer programs, but is most powerful when it involves interaction.	Learning environments should provide a multitude of social artifacts and interactions, such as those provided in interactive computer programs and cooperative learning.	The Web allows for expanded interactions on a social plane, for children to use the same tools used by experts (e-mail exchange with experts, Web publishing, etc.). It also expands the opportunity for interpersonal exchange as well as intrapersonal exchange through feedback that promotes **self-assessment**.

(Continued)

Table 2.1 (Continued)

Theory or Finding	Inference for Curriculum and Assessment	Technology Advantage
The actions and connections required in the construction of new knowledge involve several levels of brain function including metacognitive controls and the retrieval and processing of prior knowledge.	Learning environments should provide for experiences that stimulate or connect to prior knowledge and metacognitively help the student form new algorithms or generalizations.	Technology can assist the teacher in creating the stimuli that connect to prior knowledge, and it can use a multitude of visual and auditory scaffolds to help students form new generalizations.
	The curriculum should respond to **diagnosed differences** in students' learning strategies, experience, and goals.	Technology allows for careful **assessments** to measure progress toward meeting standards.
Intelligence is a multiple construct. It may include tactual, logical-mathematical, spatial, and musical differences. The individual's ability to construct new knowledge and solve problems may be a factor of the function of each of these levels or areas of brain function as well as a factor of the previous experience and goals.	Curriculum should provide opportunities for students to achieve satisfaction and a sense of power in their high-skill areas, but it should also stretch their lower-performance areas.	Technology offers the teacher an opportunity to provide and **assess** a varying level of experiences and easily accessed alternatives that address them.

their artwork, and watching them perform in an historical drama may be more convincing and more meaningful. New York is one of several states that publish school report cards as well. Parents can compare their school's performance with others. Many critical family decisions may be made based on the published results of HSSB tests. We must ensure the validity of the measures and their meaning in the total context!

And this brings us to the virtual nature of the Internet. We all have to learn new information-filtering skills, skills that were always necessary but are more so now that the forms of communication are so expanded. We need to learn how to evaluate what others say. We cannot accept everything on the Internet as truth. It doesn't even have a librarian to help screen the stuff we see. Because it is virtual, we still need teachers to make the decisions about when and how to use technologically based experiences and information, and we still need the human, social, learning requirement of face-to-face interaction with other human beings. Even the techies flock to computer conferences, and my computer scientist daughter prefers a phone call to e-mail. Most students prefer to have a friend at their side as they explore the world with their computers. Teachers can read this book, access the curriculum standards and units of many states, and find sample HSSB test questions. State education departments usually supply these. For example, readers may try www.emsc.nysed.gov/ciai/assess.html (retrieved January 30, 2002). As they implement the standards that others may have agreed on and that they have been given responsibility for, however, teachers will still need to use real spoken words; smiles of understanding, approval, and satisfaction; quizzical looks of confusion; and other human exchanges as they learn with each other and prepare their students to cross the assessment bridge.

SOME CONCLUSIONS ABOUT TECHNOLOGY IN THE CLASSROOM

Nevertheless, teachers have to accept the responsibility to prepare all students for life in the 21st century. The workplace demands that employees can independently solve problems and access the vast sources of electronic information. Beyond that, life itself will demand knowledge access skills, and the level of skills individuals possess will have a profound effect on the quality of their lives. What must schools do to prepare their students to participate in the technological life of the next century—to compete in future social, academic, and workplace endeavors?

Computers and wiring have been installed in schools at a constantly accelerating pace; it is now imperative that the human infrastructure be built at the same pace. The human infrastructure ultimately has to be progenerative (self-renewing), but as we set it into place, we recognize that the construction of this human component will place more demands than ever on classroom teachers and their leaders. They are the first line in the construction of the human component. We offer the following recommendations as a process for reaching the goal of a competent, school-based human infrastructure to help prepare our coming generation for the present and future:

1. Teachers need to learn to use technology in ways that support new practices. This first line of action will have to strengthen the skills of preservice and in-service teachers to

   • Provide a technology-rich classroom environment that works for all students—to a level that may have to compensate for missing components in the home
   • Engage in constant reflective and creative curriculum construction that is responsive to the rapid pace of technological innovation

   At the teacher education level, some institutions, including my own, have developed standards or goals in reference to the applications of technology, and some have even set up competency testing. Hill and Somers (1996) describe the process by which goals were developed at the University of Georgia but remind us that "Technological tools in the classroom lose meaning without consideration of the basic nature of the teaching-learning process" (p. 305). Technology can present new ways of thinking about the learning process that transcend issues of integrating it into instruction. It can speak to the broader issue of educational reform that ensures teaching for understanding for all children. One of the most significant impacts of the use of computers in the classroom is change in teaching style. Teachers can go beyond the traditional information delivery mode, where they are presenters of ready-made knowledge, and become facilitators of students' learning.

2. Teachers must be involved in the construction of technology-based curriculum. The concept of teachers' role in their own development and that of their colleagues needs to be engaged. Teachers must act as, and must see themselves as, valued and active participants in their own professional growth. Teacher training should nurture the development of new visions. Technology can be a vital part of that vision development for students about to become teachers; learning how to use it can help it keep the practicing teachers' visions new and revitalized. Like their students, teachers learn the best when they are confronted with problem tasks, especially when a problem's solution requires the

creation of a new product, such as curriculum that incorporates new knowledge.

3. Technology must be grounded firmly in standards-based curriculum, both as a content area unto itself and as a tool for helping students learn other subject matter content. Absent this grounding, which too often is neglected in the rush to glittery application, changes in student performance are unlikely.

4. Teachers have to be ready for the challenge. In order to make learning happen and overcome some of the hurdles that exist in conventional classrooms, we need teachers who understand and can manage the variables in the environment that have been proven to affect learning. Teachers must set high expectations and use the tools of technology to help them create learning environments that minimize rote instruction and encourage exploration, problem solving, and discovery—environments in which students actively construct their knowledge. Implementation of a technology-rich, constructivist, and learning-research informed curriculum in the classroom, by the most capable teachers, may be a critical part of the solution to the achievement gap—to the discrepancy between the haves and the have-nots. Learning how to use technology and using it to learn, however, are necessary skills for every participant in the culture of our present and future (see Chapter 6).

3 Taking the First Steps Toward Productive Change

ABOUT THIS CHAPTER

Now that, as bridge builders, we have examined solutions to the problems of underachieving schools already proposed by others, we can begin to consider our own. Our solutions should draw on effective elements tried by others but, in addition, reflect the insights and knowledge of our own experience. In this chapter, the assessment bridge construction process will begin with an examination of the variables of change that need to be considered. Although we have already examined the particular variables of history and setting that frame the starting place for school reform, we will revisit them to see how they might function in the change process. This will be followed by some general suggestions for the first steps in building the undergirding structures of piers or towers, which may be needed to support the final road surfaces of our bridge. Included in our view of the support systems are the necessary variables of capacity, ownership, leadership, and time.

THE VARIABLES OF CHANGE

There have been many attempts to identify the concepts of change and bring them into the consensual domain—or generate ideas that most of us would agree on. I feel most comfortable with a set of human and situational variables that have, over time, demonstrated to others as well as to me their power to affect the school change process.

Spady and Marshall (1990) have defined the variables of vision, capacity, ownership, and support as generic bases of transformation in schools. Based on my own and others' experience with change, I have added time, the power of leadership support and pressure, and history and setting to this list. None of the variables are independent; they all interact, but the variable of time may be an overarching control of each of them. I find it useful to separate these variables into three categories: the background variables of history, vision, and voice; the action path variables of building capacity and generating ownership; and, in the third category, the overarching variable of time.

VISION AND VOICE

Vision, according to Spady and Marshall (1990), allows us to use a picture of the future to decide what our actions in the present should be. If a vision is present and consistent, it can provide direction for change. There are two critical qualifiers to the importance of vision: A vision must represent the voices of those for whom the vision is intended (Goodson, 1992), and the nature of the change it proposes must be convincing. Most of us have a vision of what could be—perhaps not always a precise goal, but a "view of a realistic, credible, attractive future" (Bennis & Nanus, 1985, p. 89). If that vision provides direction for your own life, it can be of great value. If your vision implies common goals and impacts the lives of others, it may have even greater value—unless, of course, you neglect to allow the others a voice (Goodson, 1992).

Successful transfer of your vision to those who will be affected by it may depend on its nature and your ability to convince others of its worth, but it will also be affected by your willingness to listen and respond to their voices. For this reason, I refer to the person or group that motivates others to change as the evocator of change; the *evocator* calls forth from others and listens.

Schools often make the mistake of either isolating themselves from the greater societal ethos or responding impetuously to its ephemeral bubbles and blips. They present a vision of their own that is in conflict with the way most people are thinking, or ignore the vision evoked by a politician or media anxious for attention. In the current instance, schools cannot make this mistake. The voices are loud and clear—and there are serious sanctions threatened for not listening.

HISTORY AND SETTING

The events that comprise the initiation of systemic change can be construed as the building of new settings, but they are usually built on an old foundation. Just as visions project the future, history looks at the past. Sarason (1972) has reminded us that "confronting its [the setting's] history for the purpose of dealing with it was crucial for its future" (p. 63). Even the present, which seems so apparent to us, is, in effect, the result of the past, and so there is also a need to begin the building of new settings with a critical and in-depth analysis of the present. It may provide a rationale for that confrontation. Careful attention to history and setting prepares a system for successful implementation of change, and history itself can mitigate success. I began my analysis of history and setting in the preceding chapter and will refer to it as I proceed.

BOUNDED RATIONALITY

A good example of how history and setting can affect the process of change is to examine the possible sources of some of the recent protests against mandated tests as requirements for graduation in Massachusetts and New York. In an interesting proposal for evaluating educational reforms, House (1996, pp. 6-7) recommends that we examine reform suggestions in terms of three factors taken from transaction cost economic analysis; he suggests that these factors may affect the reform adoption and success rate. The first factor is "bounded rationality"—the reality that not everyone understands everything in a rational manner. When the Massachusetts Board of Education declared that by 2003 the Massachusetts Comprehensive Assessment System (MCAS) exam would be required for graduation, a petition with 7,000 signatures called for the law's repeal. Protestors in May 2000 included the National Association for the Advancement of Colored People (NAACP) and the American Civil Liberties Union (ACLU) as well as teachers, parents, and students from urban school districts (Cochran-Smith, 2000; Hayward, 2000). Apparently, what the legislature saw as a way to improve the instruction of minority students by holding teachers accountable, protestors saw as a device that "punishes students." Students nicknamed the MCAS the "Massachusetts Conspiracy Against Students."

In response, the Massachusetts Board of Education is reviewing findings from a task force that ordered the creation of an appeals process so high school students who narrowly fail the state exam could still receive diplomas. Education Commissioner David Driscoll reasoned that an educationally sound and fair appeals process for the graduation requirement would be essential to determining competency with integrity (Hayward, 2001).

Under the proposal, a student with passing grades who took the MCAS exam and its retests and scored between 200 and 220 would have the right to ask local school officials to file an appeal, Hayward reports. School officials would screen appeal requests before forwarding them to a regional appeals board. The regional appeals board would review documentation that shows

MCAS effort, good attendance, and demonstration of 220-level work in classroom projects or on other standardized tests in math and English. The regional board then would forward their recommendations to the commissioner's office, where final approval would be granted.

OPPORTUNISM AND ASSET-SPECIFIC INVESTMENTS

The second factor suggested by House (1996) is "opportunism," or the reality that people choose courses of action based on the promise of personal gain. In June 1999, the Massachusetts speaker of the house caused 20,000 teachers to march in protest when, while trying to make a point with his constituents for testing, he referred to teachers as "idiots"; the story was reported by Vigue and Daley in the June 17, 1999, *Boston Globe* article, "20,000 Teachers on the March Give State House a Message" (as cited in Cochran-Smith, 2000, p. 259). Anxious about this disparaging attitude, proposed teacher tests and retraining requirements if their students failed, teachers then seized on the opportunity to join parents and students in protest of the MCAS tests (Cochran-Smith, 2000, p. 261).

House's third factor is that it is not easy to implement change in educational settings because teachers' already acquired skills are "asset specific," and they have already sunk time and energy in them. Several New York City magnet schools, and the Westchester suburban Scarsdale district, had made sizable recent investments in the development of portfolio assessments as alternatives for high school graduation. The state education department had encouraged these alternatives, and suddenly they were discounted.

The preceding scenarios are common, often repeated in just the same tone in our country's schools, as teachers try to come to a consensus and comply with the call for higher standards and greater uniformity in the school curriculum. Perhaps, as a manifestation of bounded rationality, teachers who seem to have little trouble planning day-to-day activities for their students, and who can usually also state desired goals or standards in a general way, have difficulty translating the generalities into more specific expectations. Aligned activities that lead toward the accomplishment of the goals are also more difficult. Choices of activities are usually loosely connected to the content standards but are frequently based on other criteria, such as accessibility, student control and interest factors, and public relations appeal. For example, worksheets are easy to obtain and use; they control the children and document and advertise the curriculum to a parent and supervisory audience. This makes them asset-specific (and comfortable) investments. By design, they mimic the standardized tests that are used as measures of our own performance as well as the children's and are, therefore, opportunistic.

All three of House's factors apply in varying ways to the communities who must now face the reality of high-stakes testing. There is bounded rationality in their understanding of the consequences and the advantages, perhaps because these vary from place to place. There is opportunism in the fact that community members use information about schools to make high-stakes decisions about where to purchase a home or relocate a business. Certainly, those already living in a community are concerned about how previously private, negative information about schools will affect their present assets.

Among the existing assets of public education today is the capacity of the present systems. In 2001 to 2002, over 90% of American children will attend public schools at a cost of $330 billion. The average length of schooling has increased from less than 82 days in 1776 to 14½ years today. In 1950, only 13.7% of African Americans over 18 had a high school education, compared with 77.6% today (Salomon, 2001). The schools still have a distance to go in building new and improved capacity, but not taking advantage of, and making connections to, already existing capacity would be a mistake. The first step in building our new assessment bridge is to construct the piers or towers of new capacity, but it may be judicious to use the already existing resources.

STEP ONE: BUILDING NEW CAPACITY

Spady and Marshall (1990) describe the building of new capacity as the renewal or acquisition of new knowledge, skills, and orientations, which may require giving some things up while retaining and integrating what must be continued. Once capacity is attained and new practices are comfortably assimilated, they drive reflective practice. Clarity in the curriculum, consensus on the desired outcomes, and authenticity in our assessments help us gain capacity and power—the power that comes with feelings of success and ability to control. Capacity is a significant action path variable in the change process; its growth and maintenance require time and the energies of teachers and their leaders.

In his comments on the move to high-stakes testing, former Assistant Secretary of Education Kent McGuire (2000) makes the following comment recognizing existing capacity:

> We should be careful not to make educational decisions that will have major impact on an individual child based on a single test score . . . and for the most part teachers know how complicated the lives of most children are. Schools understand that student test score data must be combined with other information when deciding about retention or promotion or access to special learning opportunities. (p. 290)

McGuire then continues, however, with the schools' responsibility for gaining new capacity with this suggestion: "Judgments need to be made about curriculum and instruction, expanded learning opportunities before and after school, developing the talents of teachers and even improving the quality of assessments used to measure performance" (p. 290).

We will return to the specifics of building new capacity in greater detail in Chapter 6. The result of new capacity should be ownership.

STEP TWO: GENERATING OWNERSHIP

When an element of knowledge, a value, attitude, or practice feels as though it belongs to you and is not something imposed on you by someone else, you have ownership of it. History and its result, the present setting, are often the variables that impede the assumption of ownership by those affected by change, especially when it disrupts traditional roles; but knowledge of setting and making connections to it can be positive guiding forces toward change— a starting place. Connecting new knowledge to previous experience is as effective in the change process as it is in the learning process. Ownership of new practices can require the abandonment of old ones, and shifts in ownership create interim loss of comfort. New ownership of state-mandated accountability measures can be facilitated by increasing the clarity and alignment of current curriculum and instructional materials with the tests—and with greater teacher input into the form, quality, and consequences of the tests.

Most of the past literature on the change process refers to the phase in which a given change becomes part of the culture as institutionalization—a rather cold and formal word. In relationship to the school as a system, I prefer Fullan's (1994) term, *reculturization,* because it recognizes the power of the underlying informal culture. Reculturization is the roadway of our bridge to ownership. In terms of the individual teacher who forms that culture and must gain new capacity, I suggest a metaphor of digestion, absorption, and assimilation. The new practice has to be digested into understandable and connectable bits, absorbed, and then reconstituted or assimilated into a new personal form. The assimilation stage makes a new idea or method a habit of practice, one that feels comfortable and brings satisfaction and reward—it creates ownership.

Ultimate ownership of a new idea may require documentation. For educators, the form of this documentation is the written curriculum standards and assessments. For curriculum to have the greatest meaning to you as an individual teacher, you may first need to say it, write it in your own words, and confirm it with your students and, perhaps, with your peers. Then you may want to measure your accomplishment of it on your terms, or as it has meaning to you and, hopefully, your students.

For curriculum to have meaning for a culture, other stakeholders must be considered and contracts made or consensus reached; but those contracts need only be in terms of the content outcomes to be achieved. These are the outcomes measured by mandated tests. Individual teachers, however, still need the power and freedom to respond creatively to their situation-bound exigencies. They are on safe ground if their own measures match those of the larger culture. Written connections are the most useful because they provide the documented frames of reference, evidence, and rewards for change.

STEP THREE: ASSUMING LEADERSHIP

Leadership within schools is most often associated with boards of education and administrators. Good administrative leaders can use their power to control others—but they can also give power to others with their support and by facilitating the growth of capacity. Similarly, teachers in the classroom value power or control over students, where teachers are the leaders, and anything that diminishes their classroom control or power is threatening. Notwithstanding this need to be in charge, their ultimate leadership goal is to support their students in the acquisition of the power of new knowledge.

Support by leaders has often been linked with its counterpart, pressure. Support and pressure by leaders are energy-requiring manifestations of power. Pressure needs the company of support, and it differs from support only in the way power is managed. Administrators, teachers, and government officials need power to provide the actions of support and pressure as needed. The possession of power, however, does not guarantee the appropriate actions for productive change. Like the electric power in our lines, it has potential, but it must be delivered to the appropriate machine or encounter resistance to do its work. Government officials have the power to make laws that impact schools, but until the laws the officials make pressure schools into action with sanctions or support them with funds, the power has no effect.

As recent events have demonstrated, leadership for changing schools can come from many sources: politicians, government agencies, school administrators, outside individuals and groups, or individual teachers and their peer groups. Among these sources of leadership, the exchange of power can be multidirectional. For example, teachers who use power to improve the test scores of students not only give the students power but, concurrently, increase their own power and, subsequently, perhaps, the power of the politician who encouraged the test. In a more subtle exchange of power, reflections by individual teachers or by peer groups can be the source of pressure and support on teachers themselves, but exchanges of power can also be a source of leadership for change that creates pressure or provides support for administrators. No matter what the source, those who are led need the security that comes from consistency in the direction or vision of leadership. One of the major obstacles to a smooth transition for current accountability measures is lack of consistent leadership. We will make specific suggestions for the provision of leadership in the final chapter.

STEP FOUR: PROVIDING TIME FOR LEARNING AND CHANGE

Time is our final and overarching identified variable. It is needed first as a resource to accomplish change. Time must be purposely allocated for professional development and curriculum construction. Time must be considered in relationship to the *zeitgeist* or the timeliness of the change. One must ask the question, "Is this the right time to do this?" Finally, time matters as the fourth dimension through which we must travel as change occurs. All individuals must replace their own previous constructs with new ones—disequilibrium may need to come first. It takes time for people to construct and take ownership of new cultures and their own new knowledge, and they and their environments may again change over time.

Our experience with the process of change has confirmed these observations about time. Time has always been a significant but underestimated variable in our efforts to improve schools. In many cases, our impatience, while in the process of change, takes over without regard either for the chaos and uncertainty, or for the power, of the vast and different forces that need to be understood and dealt with before order can come.

The actions of change require energy that must come from all who are involved in the process, but they require time as well. More than that, they may be governed by time; and it is important to understand the intensity of its influence. Based on his experience as an external change agent (evocator) helping to restructure three California elementary schools, Donohue (1993) comes to several conclusions about the impact of time. Included among these is the realization that restructuring schools involves formal rearrangement of the use of time to allow them to create and sustain the kind of interactive culture and supporting infrastructure needed to improve student learning.

An equally insightful and comprehensive report to the secretary of education by the National Education Commission on Time and Learning (1994) considers time an overall and critical limiting factor in school reform. Its report is, in fact, titled *Prisoners of Time,* and it calls time the schools' warden. Although I do not believe that time is quite that simply the sole variable of restructuring and reculturization, it is so significant in terms of its many aspects that I have found it useful to consider time an overarching variable needing consideration of its effect on each of the others.

Teachers in the United States often identify the lack of time as a resource as a constraint. They complain simultaneously of the lack of time for instruction of required curriculum and of their own lack of time for professional activities other than the direct instruction of students. Although this would appear to be a conundrum, careful analysis of how the time is spent reveals where the solutions might lie. Comparisons of time usage in the United States and in Japan, which outperformed this country on the TIMSS test, reveal that overall time spent by students on the subjects of math and science may actually be less than the reported time in this country (Linn, Lewis, Tsuchida, & Songer, 2000). There is, however, a decided difference in how that time is spent. For example, fewer topics are covered but are covered more intensely in Japan, and uninterrupted periods of academic concentration are regularly interspersed with periods of play and exercise. There is also a significant difference in the structure of lessons, which we will discuss in Chapters 5 and 6.

Only about half the Japanese teachers' daily 8 or 9 school hours are actually spent instructing students. In contrast, instruction typically occupies more than two thirds of the school day for American teachers. German teachers are generally through with school shortly after noon, and the short instructional day in Germany leaves teachers with time for cooperative planning and professional development. The need for time for professional development to prepare teachers for HSSB tests cannot be underestimated. In their anxiety for a quick fix for the nation's schools, our leaders may have overlooked a significant variable of change. A sufficient time period for reculturization and assumption of ownership of higher and common standards before the testing began might have eliminated unnecessary stress on our humanly sensitive systems of education.

CHANGING SCHOOLS IN THE SEARCH FOR A BETTER FUTURE

It is my belief that attempts at educational change in the past have often been scuttled by lack of attention to one or all the variables listed in the preceding section. Educators' visions of change were rare or limited to minor aberrations: a superficially new curriculum, an adjustment in schedule or organization. Politicians' visions paid little attention to the variety of voices, the setting, and history, or to the need to develop new capacity for those required to implement these innovations. Ownership was difficult to attach to teachers who had no power or control over what was formally or legally imposed. They overcame pressure by resorting instead to more comfortable and familiar, informal choices behind closed doors. Leadership support was erratic and inconsistent, limited to materials or the sometimes inflexible and threatening supervision of administrators. And never was there enough time.

These disadvantages do not gainsay that every innovative attempt is unique and subject to the different pressures of different cultures and conditions. Although my primary focus for gleaning insights and generalizations about school improvement via the assessment bridge is a personal adventure, I attempt to include connections, as well, to the insights and experiences of others. Readers may also connect to their own previous adventures. My purpose for sharing these insights with readers is that in their ventures into using assessment for school improvement, they have the benefit of having been informed of the nature and possible causes of successes and failures. They will, however, have to construct their own new knowledge.

The hoped-for benefit for children and our future society, which may be derived from the current wave of school reform, is still to be determined. Clear statements of standards and carefully articulated measures of the achievement of these standards may have productive results if applied in the context of history and setting, with careful attention to building new capacities and ensuring ownership. Measures will have to separate the effects of schooling from the effects of home and peers. Time and leadership will be needed. Schools must be willing to accept responsibility for what they and their teachers achieve.

My greatest anxiety, however, is that top-down imposition of untested sanctions on a tried, mostly successful system of public education will create a backlash that will take down all the possible benefits of clarity in the expectations and a reasonable measure of accountability for the American curriculum. As there is for the rats soaking up the oil with their tails, there may be some temporary benefits, but a front-ended approach provides the meat and potatoes that last. The remaining chapters suggest a plan for avoiding such a consequence.

4 The Assessment Roadway: How Tests Tell Us What to Do

ABOUT THIS CHAPTER

An obvious and stated reason for the focus on government-mandated assessments as a means for making schools better is the recognition of the validity of the aphorism "What gets tested gets taught." Tests can drive the curriculum (Resnick & Resnick, 1989). My own experience with similar tests casts little doubt on their power to quickly and inexpensively (in terms of public funds) generate significant change. The quality, desirability, and longevity of the tests and the changes they induce will be determined over time. Nevertheless, even in the interim, appropriate and constructive responsive actions by schools and individual teachers may be highly productive. If improperly responded to, however, high-stakes, standards-based (HSSB) tests can also narrow our curriculum and call our attention, energy, and resources away from what may be more important but not directly tested.

Consequently, a lasting and useful roadway foundation for our assessment bridge can be a set of program-improving responses to the current reality of distally produced measures. For example, disaggregated analysis of test scores, which separates the holistic data into subscores based on affecting internal or external variables, can give us valuable clues about causes and

Table 4.1   The Six Critical Actions Directed at Building Capacity
and Ownership of HSSB Tests

1. All affected individuals (school administrators, teachers, parents, and
   students) should gain a clear understanding of the role of HSSB tests
   in the context of the school environment, state standards, school
   curriculum, and the individual child.
2. Combined or holistic scores on HSSB tests need to be carefully
   disaggregated to show individual and group variations within the whole.
   Disaggregated data can reveal the relationships between test scores and
   variables such as gender, socioeconomic status, and race—and even
   environmental variables such as teacher experience and attitude, time,
   and curriculum. Tests that use evaluative rubrics should also be
   disaggregated to determine the levels of concept mastery.
3. Each item should be examined to search for consensus on the
   embedded concepts it seeks to measure.
4. The school curriculum needs to be examined to search for alignment with
   these concepts.
5. Consensus on the necessary curriculum adjustments must be reached.
6. Preservice teacher education and professional development for in-service
   teachers must provide practitioners with a knowledge base of articulated
   and appropriate learning experiences.

effects, and suggest remedies. The articulation of HSSB tests with curriculum
can direct us in the choices we make for our everyday instructional activities
and in our in-action reflections on the progress of individual students.
Another productive response may be the construction of proximal assessments
that measure the same concepts identified in the distal one.

In these next steps in our bridge-building process, we will begin by examining the role of HSSB tests as one important measure among several informing sources of the assessment process. This will be followed by suggestions for how the results of HSSB tests can guide us toward school improvement. In order to be truly informing and effective, six critical actions (Table 4.1) directed at building capacity and ownership (change variables previously discussed must be undertaken by proximal groups of affected individuals).

This chapter addresses the specifics of the first two actions. It will place the currently recommended tests in the context of the overall process of assessment, and then bring us greater detail of the purpose, methods, meaning, and role of score disaggregation in framing instruction. Chapter 5 will address actions 3, 4, & 5, and Chapter 6 will address action 6.

DEMONSTRATING KNOWLEDGE

In a previous book, I used the theater as a metaphor for creating the classroom environment. The heart of that metaphor is that like the theater, the learning and teaching process is an ongoing demonstration of knowledge to others. Even as they are constructing their own new personal knowledge and evaluating themselves, much of what students and their teachers do in schools is for the purpose of demonstrating to others. On the classroom stage, the teacher and student performers constantly demonstrate to each other what they know, and productively use the performances to help direct and motivate further actions. These performances are at the heart of what we refer to as informal assessment. Schools, however, also have other off-stage and demanding audiences: parents and the public at large, for whom they must demonstrate that the time and resources spent on education are effective. Like good theater, a well-communicated demonstration for others, whether it is within the action on stage or directed toward the audience, sometimes involves putting on a special face or mask. That special face in our current culture of schools is in the form of standardized, and now HSSB, tests.

When demonstrations go beyond the purpose of communicating with immediately present others and are measured and compared to a standard, they become quality or quantity indicators of what the performer knows, has accomplished, or can do. And then we also need to determine how students will demonstrate the intended knowledge (McTighe, 1996). Because they have different standards or criteria, theater critics and teachers often disagree on the same performance. They are not alone in their disparity.

The protests and state test boycott initiated by the Scarsdale, New York, parents (see Chapter 2) were inspired by some school staff members who communicated a lack of cohesion between the content of the test and the district's innovative curriculum. This country has had a long history of debate among those who believe that some individual rights supersede the mandates of government—even when the purpose of those mandates is to protect the many. Fortunately, our democratic system has been able to solve these differences with discussion that leads to consensus or compromise. This is where we need to go with HSSB tests.

DEFINING STANDARDS AND ASSESSMENT

Among those who have power over schools and among educators themselves, there is disagreement about what should be measured and how and why it should happen. Let us begin with the meaning of the terms *assessment* and *standard*. Tyler (Horowitz, 1995; Tyler, 1949) uses *evaluate* and *assessment* alternately. He applies *evaluate* to diagnoses of individuals and to applications for planning and curriculum but then uses the term *assessment* when addressing measures of larger groups for the purpose of informing the public. Cronbach (1963) was one of the first to describe all kinds of measures as assessment.

Wiggins (1995) also uses the term *assessment* more inclusively. He, furthermore, has defined *standard* in the singular as "an exemplary performance serving as a benchmark"; in the plural as "specific and guiding pictures"; and, when modified to *high standards,* as "a set of mature, coherent, and consistently applied values" (p. 189). In its current applications, *content standard* is ascribed to descriptions of desired ends for students that answer the question, "What should students know or be able to do?" Many originally published national and state standards documents usually begin with the statements of more general principles of knowledge or values to be attained as "content standards" but then extend these in a design-down process to make them more specific and attached to a demonstrated performance (Solomon, 1998). Some states have, in addition, followed the original standards documents with more specific curricula based on the standards.

Another form of standard statement, *performance standard,* is intended as a clearly discriminated level of the bar or model of acceptable performance. The performance standard is a translation of the content standard that additionally provides an expectation level and answers the question, "How good is good enough?" Some confusion about the application of the two related terms, *content standard* and *performance standard,* reigns because of the overlap of skill-defining terms found in performance standard statements and similar statements that respond to the skill-defining, second part of the content standard definition (what students should be able to do). Adding to the confusion, some standards documents have chosen to use the term *performance indicator.* These usually are the skill-defining parts of content standards and do not have embedded levels of attainment. The widely adopted standards of the National Council of Teachers of Mathematics (1989, 2000) and many state documents are more representative of skill-defining content standards.

The science standards of the National Research Council (NRC) (1996) are more explicit of the "knowing" content but also address the "doing" in their sections on inquiry skills and science and technology. Both documents have sections on assessment, and the NRC has a particularly well-developed chapter that provides samples and an explanation of the use of rubrics.

RUBRICS

For the purpose of meaningful assessment of student performance, the standards or performance indicators need to be translated into rubrics. In contrast to the unconstructed response on a multiple-choice test, where the correct answer is only one possible choice, a student-constructed response on a performance test needs to be interpreted. A rubric is an assessment tool that verbally describes and scales levels of student achievement on performance tasks, but it can also be associated with more conventional alphanumeric and numeric scores or grades. Rubrics describe the performed behaviors that mark the intervals or comparative characteristics and provide evidence of

Table 4.2   A Task-Specific Rubric

Skill	Above Standard	At Standard	Below Standard
Use of simple machines	Involves more than 4 kinds of machines	Involves 3 to 4 kinds of simple machines	Involves fewer than 3 kinds of machines
Understanding of simple machines	Can clearly and in detail explain how it works	Can generally explain how it works	Has difficulty explaining how it works
	Can clearly and in detail explain how it helps us do work	Can generally explain how it helps us do work	Has difficulty explaining how it helps us do work

SOURCE: Adapted from Egeland (1997, p. 45).

Performance Standard: Given the task of solving a series of problems requiring the use of machines, student will involve 3 to 4 kinds of simple machines, explain how each works and how the machine helps us work.

achievement. The descriptions can be defined as a set of guidelines for distinguishing between performances or products of different quality. Rubrics should be composed of scaled descriptive levels of progress toward an end result, which is based on the stated content standard. Thus the standard level or end result description of performance in a rubric can be written as a performance standard, which is precisely articulated with the content standard. Rubrics may also have levels above the stated, standard end result.

Depending on purposes and the standards being assessed, teachers use several different forms of rubrics. A report by the Council of Chief State School Officers (1995) defines three basic types: task specific, developmental, and relative, but there are variations and combinations. Their report also identifies strengths and weaknesses.

We will now look at these three types of rubrics.

THE TASK-SPECIFIC RUBRIC

The task-specific rubric (Table 4.2) is the most explicit in terms of its connection to a stated outcome but is limited in its application to single tasks rather than to overall objectives or standards. It is one that can easily be shared with students, but the negative descriptors may have to be changed. In the table, the standard level is highlighted and rewritten as a performance standard.

THE DEVELOPMENTAL RUBRIC

The developmental rubric is designed to assess a progression of knowledge or skill acquisitions. The advantage of the developmental rubric over the task-specific rubric is that in addition to providing some specificity, it can

Table 4.3   A Developmental Rubric: Class Participation Criteria Checklist

Level	Speaking/Reasoning	Listening
4 Above Standard	• Understands questions before answering • Cites appropriate evidence from background information • Expresses complete thoughts • Displays logic and insight • Synthesizes ideas	• Pays close attention and records details • Responses include comments of others • Identifies logical errors • Overcomes distractions
3 Standard	• Responds to questions voluntarily • Comments indicate thought and reflection • Ideas draw interest from others	• Generally pays attention • Responds thoughtfully to others • Questions logical structures • Only self-absorption may at times distract from the ideas of others
2 Approaching Standard	• Responds when called on • Comments indicate little effort in preparation • Comments may be illogical and may ignore important details • Ideas may not relate to previous comments	• Attention wavers • Classifies ideas inappropriately • Requires inordinate repetition of questions • Shows interest only in own ideas
1 Below Standard	• Extremely reluctant to participate • Comments are illogical and meaningless • Has incomplete thoughts • Makes few relationships between comments and text	• Acts uninvolved in discussion • Misinterprets previous comments and ideas • Shows ambivalence toward any ideas presented

SOURCE: University of the State of New York (1997).

Performance Standard: In interactive classroom communications, the student responds to questions voluntarily, makes comments that indicate thought and reflection, expresses ideas that draw interest from others.

Performance Standard: In interactive classroom communications, the student generally pays attention, responds thoughtfully to others, questions logical structures; only self-absorption may at times distract from the ideas of others.

assess steps toward concept mastery and has a much broader applicability, which can then be collated into holistic scores. The first example in Table 4.3 is excellent for a broad-based application to participation or oral-communication skill standards.

Table 4.4   A Developmental Math Rubric

Level 1	Level 2	Level 3	Level 4
Procedural Exploration	**Concept Mastery**	**Conceptual and Procedural Mastery**	**Application Mastery**
Can solve problems based on this concept using the real or concrete representative materials, but unable to explain concept	Can solve problems and explain the concept used, but may still need concrete material	Can generalize the concept and use related procedures, including algorithms, to solve problems without concrete material	Can generate an original problem using concept or apply it in an unusual way

Individual Assessment of Levels		
Concept	*Expected Level for Grade*	*Student's Level*
17. (See standard list)	Level 1	Level 2
18. (See standard list)	Level 3	Level 4

Performance Standard: In problem applications of concept 18 (as described and numbered in a shared, separate list of curriculum concepts), student generalizes the concept and can apply procedure and algorithms without referring to concrete materials. Or in collated form: In problem applications of concepts 17 and 18, student has attained the expected level of development.

The second example in Table 4.4 of a developmental rubric can be applied as a general rubric that corresponds to a detailed list of curriculum standards or their embedded concepts, such as the samples from mathematics in Tables 5.1 and 5.2. It requires previously shared and numbered concepts and is based on four levels of concept attainment, which are the same for each different concept. The developmental progression is based on the premise that the complete and correct construction of a concept may take time—even spanning several grades—and the length of time may differ for different students and different concepts. This does not preclude the possibility that for some concepts and students, progress through all levels can happen in a single experience.

In reporting on individual student achievement, the expected level for the grade is reported alongside the achieved level, indicating where remediation may be necessary. Since the levels are the same for each concept, a collated score of standard achievement can be computed for holistic purposes and then also disaggregated to discover specific areas of group need.

Table 4.5   Two Relative Rubrics Language and Literacy

Skill	Exceeds Standard	At Standard	Below Standard
Listening Speaking/Reasoning			

Language and Literacy—Grade One: Fall, Winter, Spring

		F	W	S
Listens for meaning in discussions and conversations	Not yet In process Proficient			
Speaks easily, conveying ideas in discussions and conversations	Not yet In process Proficient			

SOURCE: Adapted from Meisels (1996/1997, p. 60).

As shown in Table 4.4, for each concept identified from the shared list, the median expectation or standard of development for the grade level can be different. In essence, based on median expectations, each student can be below, at, or above standard for each concept. For example, some students may be at level 2 (concept mastery) of the developmental sequence for one concept, but the expectation for that grade is for them to be at level 3 (algorithmic mastery), and, therefore, those students are below standard for the concept. However, some of these students may have met the grade level expectation for a different concept. If scored grades were desired, the report could be adapted to provide a numeric or alphanumeric equivalent for achievement of the standard, surpassing it, or not achieving it.

THE RELATIVE RUBRIC

The relative rubric (Table 4.5) is the easiest to design and grade, but it gives little feedback in relation to the specific expectations. In the first example, there is no explanation of what the standard is. The second example shows how just the addition of a description of the standard level can help.

USING RUBRICS IN FORMATIVE AND SUMMATIVE ASSESSMENT

Most of the emphasis on assessment, which has been created by HSSB tests, is based on the business model of bottom-line or end results, or what we educators have called summative assessment. Rubrics can also play an important role in formative assessment. Shepard (2000) reminds us that "assessment should be part of the learning process" and that we need to "make assessment more informative, more insightfully tied to learning steps" (p. 10). These steps in formative assessment can be made transparent through the identification and sharing of rubrics.

Although politicians and educators may be interested in holistic scores, it is the analytic potential of rubrics, their ability to pinpoint specific gaps or deficiencies, that may be most useful to the school improvement process. Learning is not an all or none process; neither is the acquisition of knowledge the same in all individuals. It is also an individual day-to-day event. In the interactive scaffolding process, successful teachers help their students cross the "zone of proximal development" (Vygotsky, 1978) or "zone of construction" (Steffe & D'Ambrosio, 1995). They constantly assess with questions and observations of body language and then with reassuring paraphrases or further questions to stimulate students to self-correct. Transparent, explicit criteria are needed for both teacher and student in this formative process. Rubrics become transparent when they are shared.

Reaching transparency and a comfort level with the use of rubrics may not come easily to teachers and parents who are accustomed to traditional grading systems. Delandshere and Petrosky (1998) argue against the use of assigned numerical ratings because they are subjective in that they require judgment and are incompatible with the preferred explicitness of construct-driven performance assessment and the descriptions of performance in a rubric. Brookhart (1999) counteracts this with the argument that quantifications of performance are possible and, depending on the purpose of the assessment, can be used in tandem with qualitative descriptions.

I recently attended an elementary principals' meeting where a new report card form was discussed. Anxious to focus on specific mathematics and early literacy skills, district central office personnel had listed them in detail on the new report card for grading as a relative rubric. This was to replace the previous, traditional, overall grades of excellent, satisfactory, needs improvement, and unsatisfactory for the whole subject. The district personnel argued that the only way to get teachers to focus on the specific skills was to require them to assess them. The principals were concerned because teachers had no basis for determining what the standard level was and would have great difficulty explaining the grades to parents. What they needed was a transparent rubric for each skill, but that would take time and practice.

They had simultaneously received the new mathematics curriculum map that our team of teachers had worked on over the summer. The mathematics map had very specific embedded concepts and performance indicators, but district documents for early literacy were not yet published. Districtwide professional development still had to be planned and implemented to help teachers understand and practice the assessment process using the indicators. An interim compromise decision was to use the relative rubric of above-, at-, approaching-, and below-standard for the major categories; and the traditional grades of excellent, satisfactory, and so forth, would be applied to the specific skills. I pointed out to the group that the specific-skill grades could form an interim, quantitative base for the category, with a certain number of excellent and satisfactory grades being the standard. This was just a beginning step toward construct- or concept-driven performance assessment. *Sometimes we have to construct temporary bridges between the old and the new.*

SUMMATIVE APPLICATIONS

More summatively, disaggregated test scores based on rubrics that demonstrate the exact position on the road to mastery for a particular child or group can be very informative, as we shall see in Chapter 5. Among other criteria for creating rubrics for summative applications are that:

- They are understandable to students.
- The scores of the scale are equidistant on a continuum (at least four scores are suggested).
- Descriptors are valid (test what you want them to do or know) and scores are reliable (consistent).
- The highest point (level) may be above the end result of the performance standard.
- Scores relate to empirically validated, actual levels of student performance.
- The scale types include holistic (overall performance) and analytic (dimensions) items: The assessment of a student performance should include both types.
- They make explicit to students, parents, and administrators the criteria for student achievement.
- They can be used by students to assess their own performance and the performance of other students.

Translations of rubrics to traditional numeric or alphanumeric scores can be useful in informing a public so accustomed. Given a set of performance standards, which are the standard level of a rubric based on explicit concepts, such as those connected to the developmental rubric sample above, the numeric score can be a percentage of the complete set for which the student reaches standard level. Each numeric or alphanumeric score can then be attached in rubric form to a grade. For example: Achieving standard level or above for 30 out of 35 performance standards is the equivalent of an 85% or a B+ grade.

An emphasis on a variety of performances to demonstrate knowledge is clear in the national documents and is also common to most of the state standards publications. As expressed by McTighe (1997), "A performance-based orientation requires that we think about curriculum not simply as content to be covered but in terms of *performances of understanding*" (p. 7). Well-written performance indicators and articulated rubrics are precise, up-front descriptions of what we want our students to be able to do and clearly delineate how progress can be assessed. They also tell us what needs to be on the test. Criterion referenced tests with item-matching rubrics fit this prescription better than norm-referenced tests that just compare whole scores with the average score of samples of students.

GENERATING OWNERSHIP OF TESTS

The legislation finally passed by the U.S. Congress in December 2001 mandates assessments of students in Grades 3 to 8. Initial reaction from state education leaders, already reeling with the backlash from parents and teachers in response to their own newly developed assessment programs, resulted in a compromise delay of implementation until 2005 to 2006. The current reality, however, is continued pressure for *distal* (externally produced) HSSB measures of results of teachers' efforts. Some of the resistance to accepting ownership of HSSB measures, in the face of that reality, is due to a lack of recent research that would help us identify and understand the positive and negative impact of HSSB testing on the education of our children. There is no doubt that we will soon grow to understand the effects of the tests on our children, teachers, and resources and will evaluate them in terms of their desired, bottom-line results. In the interim, however, there are elements from the history and current setting for assessment that may help us accept and use the tests productively.

REACHING CONSENSUS ON GROUP SUMMATIVE SCORES

In our discussion of rubrics, we have established the need for clarity in our expectations. As a beginning step in gaining ownership for the summative results of HSSB tests, there must be clarity in the acceptable levels of performance for the group. Usually this is based on a norm or sample of performance. Unfortunately, there has been much confusion across this country about what an acceptable level is. States have been setting passing scores at varying and arbitrary levels. For example, California decided that the passing level on its math test was 55% of the questions answered correctly, but 60% was the standard for its English test (Rothstein, 2001). In New York, the standard for an eighth-grade test administered in May 2001 was hastily predicted by sampling the performance of a few test takers, and then school districts received disappointing results based on that sample. Final test tallies revealed that the sample was incorrect in its projections, and comparisons to this sample as a norm were incorrect.

There is also doubt raised when different measures are administered and results do not agree. In North Carolina, only 20% of students passed the National Assessment of Educational Progress (NAEP) exam, but the state test found 68% of students proficient. In Massachusetts, only 20% of eighth graders passed the state science exam, but the NAEP test showed that the students were better than comparative students in every nation tested except for Singapore (Rothstein, 2001). Sometimes, confusion is the fault of unprepared, commercial test producers overwhelmed by the sudden surge of requests. The requests are also for more complicated performance-based tests. The unfortunate consequence of this lack of available expertise is that life decisions for students, teachers, and schools are being made based on inadequate or faulty measures (Henrique & Steinberg, 2001). Panels of teachers to review the tests were set up in California and Ohio. Coming to consensus about where the bookmark (passing score) should be was a difficult task for the panels, but they did finally agree on the passing scores. Unfortunately, for political reasons, the panel's recommendations for a 70% score were overruled in California. This ambivalence and wavering undermines the public confidence and discourages students and teachers.

There is always an implementation lag (Solomon, 1998) in bringing new programs to schools, and, hopefully, the difficulties with HSSB consensus building will be overcome in time. Evidence for this may be seen in states such as Michigan and Indiana where long-term involvement of teachers in the development of standards, and professional-development programs to help teachers make the necessary changes, have been effective in raising HSSB scores. Meanwhile, there may be other effective methods for gaining ownership of already imposed tests.

MATCHING DISTAL AND PROXIMAL MEASURES

Using the broader definition of assessment to include all measures of performance and the possible advantages of teacher-owned performance indicators, we need to consider the HSSB test in the context of other, more proximal measures. Teachers in the students' on-stage audience take constant informal measures within activities and classroom discourse, reflect on these measures, and then adjust the discourse or the learning environment in response. This most-important purpose for measurement has also been the most unrecognized. The performance indicators against which teachers make informal classroom assessments are not usually those stated in written form: They are more often subliminal and intuitive, based on teachers' knowledge, their prior experience with children, and their own learning experiences. They may, however, be systematized in oral-questioning patterns and in the materials within the enabling activities.

A critical step in developing ownership of distal HSSB measures may be to achieve a better match between the informal, proximal classroom assessments employed by classroom teachers in action and those of the HSSB tests and formal, written, state curricula. An important point to consider here in relation to that step is that HSSB tests for students are also high stakes for teachers. Possible sanctions, including failure to achieve tenure or transfer to a different school, are new, realistic concerns, but teachers have always measured themselves. Although they constantly assess themselves in relation to their informal assessments of students, their self and student measures usually place greater weight on the more formal HSSB assessments—probably because these can also inform a different audience: school administrators, parents, and the public at large. My reflection on history reminds me that we accepted IQ tests and used the results intensively although they were deemed unrelated to what we did; but we also used Regents exams well, because we had a sense of ownership. We knew and accepted what was on the test. Its validity was not questioned.

VALIDITY: DOES IT FIT?

A primary criterion for judging the value of any test is its validity. "Validity is the quality of an instrument to yield truthful inferences about the trait it measures" (Smith & Fey, 2000, p. 336). Does the test tell us the truth about what we want it to measure? Before we determine the validity of the instrument, however, we must have clarity in what we want. Given the reality of distally produced tests that have so much impact on both the child and the community, we need to consider curriculum validity as well as test validity. Is our curriculum valid for what is on the test? And, in contrast, do the tests omit evaluating elements we deem worthy? In consideration of our purposes for educating our children, do tests neglect those elements of the culture that we have clearly identified worthy of transmission? If it is necessary for our citizens to respect each other and be tolerant of the minor variations in our culture, do we have such performance indicators, and do the tests match our indicators? If our purpose is for students to become competent problem solvers, do our tests evaluate skill in inquiry and the individual construction of knowledge?

Although, among educators, the constructivist approach of Piaget and Vygotsky is widely appreciated by many, it has not gained substantive understanding or support outside of the academy (Firestone, Fitz, & Broadfoot, 1999). An effort to engage students in a constructivist mathematics program in one of my neighboring school districts was criticized, and almost eliminated after a brief trial, by parents who did not understand its value and purpose. Unfortunately, some teachers—who did not understand, were reluctant to change, and were concerned about newly instituted state mathematics assessments—supported them. It was only the ultimate realization that the new state assessments required students to think in ways not stressed by traditional methods, and the embarrassment of a better performance by students in a similar district, that began to make the skeptics reconsider a possible compromise. The Pearl River, New York, district that performed better was one in which constructivist mathematics had been implemented over a 10-year period with extensive vision-sharing and capacity-building support.

GENERATING OWNERSHIP: BEGIN WITH CURRICULUM-BASED PROXIMAL ASSESSMENTS

My personal experience with the school-improvement process in the Pearl River district, which was successful in the implementation of constructivist mathematics, provides strong evidence of the following necessary elements in the development of ownership by teachers of a distally produced HSSB measure:

- There must be consensus about and clarity of the curriculum that the test measures.
- Each item on the test must be correlated with that curriculum.
- The HSSB test must be seen as possessing a value other than its role as a monitoring device.
- Test data need to be disaggregated for significant variables (discussed later in this chapter).
- The HSSB results must correlate with proximally developed, criterion-referenced tests and other informal assessments.

An underlying hypothesis for these recommendations is that ownership will decrease resistance and increase the potential for teachers to use tests in more positive and educationally productive ways. Perkins (1992) posits that distal tests may have a positive effect, provided these measure the outcomes that are desired. He notes that the inherent conflict of interest for teachers when using self-made assessments is alleviated by *good* distal assessments and states that "Some external testing *liberates* teachers to pursue instruction in closer partnership with their students" (pp. 171-172). What Perkins is suggesting, I believe, is that when the tests are high stakes for both teachers and students, they are in the battle on the same side: "Let's beat this thing together," as opposed to "I challenge you." The conflict of interest, nevertheless, may be exacerbated by perceived discrepancies between teacher-owned proximal tests and HSSB distal tests and may result in a lack of confidence by teachers in their own measures. The solution to this problem is embodied in my recommendation in the chapters ahead—for specific articulation of distal, state-developed and proximal, teacher-developed tests. *Distal* and *proximal* are terms used most frequently in anatomy and are antonyms, meaning, respectively, *far away from* and *close to* a point of origin.

PREPARING FOR THE TESTS: CURRICULUM TEACHING

The current practice in most schools, in response to the frenzy created by HSSB tests, is for teachers to bombard students with practice tests. Popham (2001), however, distinguishes between preparation for a test that is *item teaching,* which focuses on practice with actual or similar test items, and preparation that is *curriculum teaching,* which is directed at the content and skills represented by the test. A beginning step toward Popham's preferred latter approach is the identification of the content and skills we want students to know and concurrent links to measures that tell us whether students know what we want them to know. The next step connects these identifications to appropriate educational experiences. We will address this task in the remaining chapters.

In my work with Pearl River teachers, we developed our own criterion-referenced test (CRT) that matched our specific, desired outcomes, because we did not believe the normed test, the California Achievement Test (CAT), which we had been using for several years, adequately assessed what we were tying to do. Each teacher-developed test item on the CRT was correlated to specific concepts in the curriculum. We continued to use the CAT as a benchmark, and, surprisingly, the bottom-line results on the two instruments compared favorably and gave us confidence to pursue our chosen direction.

I remember one significant incident distinctly. The CAT had separately scored computation and concepts parts. Our program had de-emphasized drill and practice on computation in favor of understanding, and we wanted to relieve teachers of any connected anxiety over the possible decline in student performance on computation. Consequently, for the first test administration after initiation of the new approach, we originally planned to administer only the concepts part; but several teachers wanted to try the computation as well.

The results on the concepts portion were much better than previous administrations, but, interestingly, there was no loss of skill in computation. One teacher excitedly reported that her students had accurately answered computation questions on multidigit multiplication examples that she had not even covered. When she questioned her students about how they got their answers, they replied that they had estimated them—a skill we did emphasize— and because the test was multiple choice, they picked the closest answer.

PROXIMAL MEASURES
RESPONDING TO HSSB ANALYSES

A possible productive response to this present reality of HSSB distal mea- sures may be for teachers to make their own *proximal,* informal, and reflec- tive measures more closely aligned with the curriculum expectations that are identified by careful analysis of the distal assessments. This may appear to be *item teaching,* but if the response to distal assessment is shifted *away* from the current common practice of finding and using similar questions as a basis for instruction *to* an analysis of the test questions to discover the underlying curriculum skills and concepts required, the process may be useful. Identifi- cation and analysis of the underlying concepts embedded in an assessment item that intends to measure them can clarify these for the teacher and then lead the teacher to alternate and more prescriptive ways of helping students to learn the concepts. If the distal assessment has performance-based com- ponents with items that require constructed responses (as opposed to multiple- choice answers), the teacher will also have the advantage of analyzing these to identify the bugs in student thinking (Van Lehn, 1986).

Although proximal assessments have little power to effect widespread change, their value as reflective teaching guides, and their ownership by teachers, can have long-range effects. The hypothetical effective partnership, then, is based on a necessary foundation of consensus on the curriculum and transfer of ownership of distal measures to teachers via their analysis and ultimate adaptation—not of the items, but of the concepts measured—into their own proximal measures. This, then, has the immediate and widespread change-evoking results of the distal assessment and the long-range potential of the curriculum-based proximal ones.

In Pearl River, this method of engaging teachers in the development of proximal measures as a means for generating ownership was effective and, in addition, served as a professional-growth remedy for the reality that many teachers ineffectively teach mathematics as a set of procedures, with little insight about the underlying conceptual knowledge. The summative CRT and formative measures were combined to track the progress of our program. Formative quantitative and qualitative measures were built into the day-to-day instructional activities. The documented curriculum, written by teams of teachers, included the specific underlying concepts and matching performance indicators. The indicator keyword was *verbalize* (get your students to explain what they are doing). This had the double value of allowing for in-action assessment of individual students by the teacher and reinforcing clear connections for teachers between the prescribed curriculum and the long-term summative assessment, the CRT. The teachers chose the CRT items with each item matched to a specific concept.

Subsequent, recent, professional-development activities, in which I have engaged multidistrict teachers in the process of analyzing state-mandated tests and making explicit connections between the items and their own curricula, have been equally successful in generating ownership. There are significant indications of decreased resistance to the HSSB tests as teachers begin to see the assessment less as an imposed and threatening addition to their curriculum and more as a design or planning guide—with greater attention to the underlying conceptual knowledge and with space for some autonomy over how it gets accomplished.

The ultimate, long-range measure of validity for any implementation of change strategy is in the improvement of student performance as a result of greater teacher ownership. There was a long-range improvement in Pearl River student scores and maintenance at the top. The district consistently performs among the highest-scoring schools in the state. In 1998, 100% of third and sixth graders passed the new state test. By the mid-1990s, high school students were participating and achieving in advanced courses at double the 1980s rate. In 1998, because of accelerated eighth graders, the number of students taking the first ninth-grade Regents exam was 12% higher than the number of students in the grade, and 96% of those taking the test passed. Most of the tenth graders and some of the ninth graders took the second-year exam. Interestingly, just before the state tests were implemented, a new superintendent who doubted the validity of the local CRT test administered an international one. Pearl River students outperformed students in all countries tested. In 2002, the district was one of only two school districts nationwide to receive the prestigious Malcolm Baldrige National Quality Award from President George W. Bush.

WHAT LIES BENEATH: DISAGGREGATING SCORES

Examination of total scores in relation to norms and previous test administrations in Pearl River was reassuring, but it was careful analysis of the CRT that showed us where we needed more effort. Each question on the test was designed by teachers to assess a particular concept, and we used a computer management system to indicate mastery of each concept by school, class, and individual student (see Table 4.4). Our efforts were directed at the school motto: "All children can and will learn." When deficiencies were analyzed, we shared responsive group and individualized instructional strategies at grade-level meetings. Modeling by the more experienced teachers for others was directed at ensuring that every child attained mastery. Each participating teacher received a mastery-level report on the skills of incoming students at the beginning of the year to avoid unnecessary repetition and highlight needed redevelopment. The performance-based rubrics for newly administered, state HSSB tests allow for similar disaggregation if they are attached, as we describe in Chapter 5, more specifically to the curriculum concepts. Another form of disaggregation, however, proved very enlightening and may be most useful in achieving equity for the schools across our nation.

DISAGGREGATING FOR NONINSTRUCTIONAL DIFFERENCES

In our multicultural country, it is important that we consider insights from multiple perspectives and learn, appreciate, and grow from these in ways that will contribute positively to policy, practice, and social justice. Greater understanding of the causes may help the search for ways to close the gaps between our many subcultures. Proper treatment depends on accurate diagnosis. In mathematics, we have long been concerned by the gender discrepancy, and much effort has been expended to overcome it. A report on unexpected and disappointing findings in a longitudinal study on gender differences at an early age (Fennema, Carpenter, Jacobs, Franke, & Levi, 1998) framed a variety of responses from math and gender specialists. The framing study investigated the results of reform-based mathematics that included careful emphasis on solving nonroutine problems with a variety of materials and supportive professional development for the teachers involved. The 3-year study traced the performance of first through third graders and discovered that although girls could solve problems, their strategies tended to be more conventional and less innovative. This difference can be significant in the later challenges of more complex mathematics and may be the reason for the often-measured decline in mathematics performance among adolescent girls.

The responses to the findings of the research varied. Hyde and Jaffe (1998) conjectured that the differences might be attributed to girls' tendency toward compliance and boys' inclination toward competition and risk taking. They attribute some of this to differences in early play activities and also conjecture that *reactive interactions* (p. 15) between the teacher and girls might encourage them to continue their use of traditional approaches.

The competitive-attitude difference has been demonstrated by others and by me in previous research. In 1976, I was involved in a study that investigated possible causes for the decline in SAT scores. We reached a dead end with some of the possible variables such as birth order. In a search for variables that might have explained the difference in male and female scores, however, I discovered a significantly higher attitude of competition in boys taking SAT exams. They rated the test as much more important than the girls who took it at their side. My hunch is that even in the changed culture of this new millennium, this attitude may not have changed. A recent survey investigated why women do not enter the high-paced and competitive technology fields as frequently as men. Although women make up 46% of the workforce, they account for only about 28% of high-tech jobs. The survey revealed that women rank happiness, family, and friendship as their top indicators for success. A good job, money, and power were at the bottom (Mclain, 2001).

Noddings (1998) suggests that the differences may be the result of differences in interest. She adds a disclaimer, however, and asks, "Why do we see it as a problem if young women are less interested than young men in mathematics?" (p. 17). She suggests that it is the valorizing of mathematics by society that is at fault and that although we should investigate what factors contribute to girls' interest in mathematics, we neither ignore nor devalue other interests. "No student's self-worth should depend on his or her interest in mathematics" (p. 18).

Sowder (1998) reflects on the importance of the gender differences in mathematics strategy development in its long-term effects on "deep understanding of numbers and operations" (p. 6). Her concern that the results of the Fennema et al. (1998) study not be interpreted as a failure of mathematics school reform should not be taken lightly in the context of recent pressures to "go back to basics." Sowder's call is for further research, and I add that somehow, we must do a better job of documenting and publicizing our successes.

Somewhat overlooked in the responses to the Fennema et al. research finding were some other possible variables from the larger body of research evidence on the effects of goals and motivation. Interest is just part of the motivation picture. It could very well be that girls and boys are equally wired to succeed but that their ultimate approach and success are mitigated by variations in goals. Recent definitions of constructivism place considerable emphasis on this. Von Glasersfeld's (1990) widely accepted definition implies that individuals construct new reality or knowledge based on previous knowledge and new experiences and that the construction of revised knowledge is governed by human goals. Human goals can be interpreted in terms of the affective factors such as motivation, attitude, and interest that have previously demonstrated and recognized effects on learning. Human goals are created and modified by sociocultural, interactive environments. Only part of those environments are in the classroom.

Glasser (1986) describes a control theory axiom with a trenchant metaphor in this description: "What students (and all of us) do in school (and out) is completely determined by the pictures in their heads" (p. 39).

He believes that all children come to school with a picture that school is a satisfying place and are willing to work to achieve satisfaction. Lack of success changes the pictures in their heads—and their sense of power, which he declares is a strong human need (and goal). Teachers and parents help put these pictures (and goals) in children's heads. Girls' pictures may be different when they first get to school, and they may prefer to use the conventional methods that continue to give them power.

The metacognitive factor of interest as an influence on the acquisition of new knowledge has been studied in some depth. In a review of the research literature, Tobias (1994) relates interest to prior knowledge and to the acquisition of new knowledge. He attributes lack of strong previous findings of a relationship between interest and prior knowledge to design and measurement problems and suggests further studies. Girls who are missing the prior knowledge of innovative problem-solving approaches because of differences in their informal play activities would then have less interest in mathematics problems. They also may not have had the informal work and play activities that were part of my own experience as described in Chapter 1.

The importance of informal, "doing" endeavors has been established by cross-cultural studies—sometimes comparing small, neighboring subcultures—which clearly demonstrate that the informal experiences of varied cultures create disparate abilities (e.g., Ginsburg, Posner, & Russell, 1981; Lave, 1977; Song & Ginsburg, 1987). Girls may exist in separate subcultures from boys, and although the learning is quite apart from the formal learning acquired in schools, it may have a goal-controlling impact. However, gender is not the only subculture. It may, as a matter of fact, be situated as a subculture within another.

The preceding discussion recalls some interesting data I collected as part of in-process, program evaluation activities for the Pearl River school district, which may call for a further analysis of the Fennema et al. (1998) results. Our data on student achievement were disaggregated for the variables of gender and socioeconomic status (SES). In 1987, the school district was a rather homogeneous suburb of New York, with a middle-income population that included many families of civil-service employees. Performance before reform by students in mathematics, especially at the secondary level, was well below expectations. As described, the intensive, districtwide, staff development and program activities were similar to those in the Fennema et al. study.

Table 4.6　　Three-Year Comparison: Overall Pearl River Scores

Grade	California Achievement Tests: National Percentile of Mean Score (Each Year)			CRT Mastery Level	
	Year 1	Year 2	Year 3	Year 2	Year 3
1	71.0	72.7	79.8	91	95
2	73.7	84.4	84.9	87	85
3	73.9	77.5	Not given	75	82
4	71.7	73.5	85.0	66	80

The emphasis was on an innovative, problem-solving, constructivist approach at all levels and on higher expectations for participation in math courses in high school.

The original data for overall results covered the initial 3-year period of reform efforts, and its demonstration of positive effects has been maintained and even improved over the long term. Results were particularly significant for the earlier grades, where students had experienced the new program from the beginning, and teachers had more experience as well. The data are not truly longitudinal, in that the same students were not tracked over the 3 years, but the consistency of the population over the period allows us to make some inferences. The results were not disaggregated until the end of year 2, when we felt comfortable with the overall results and began to seek answers to questions about variations among the students. The average number of students tested for each of the levels tested was about 120.

The total scores (Table 4.6) on both the Criterion Referenced Test (CRT) and the California Achievement Test (CAT) were reassuring, but the score distributions were not entirely normal. There was a double bell curve, with a group of students well above the mean and another smaller, but noticeable, group below the mean. We were anxious to discover why some groups were progressing better than others and decided to disaggregate the total scores. Gender differences were a possibility, but we also hypothesized socioeconomic variations. Because of the apparent homogeneity of the population in terms of income level, the data were also disaggregated by the mother's level of education—a previously proven socioeconomic variable. This information was also accessible because it was part of the school enrollment record. There were two categories of socioeconomic status for the first through fourth graders who took the tests. Students whose mothers had only a high school education or less were placed in the A1 category, and those whose mothers had some college were placed in the B2 category. Processing problems limited the data disaggregation to just the CAT data, but we were satisfied that the results on the CRT were congruent.

Table 4.7   California Achievement Test Percentile Scores:
                  Disaggregated by SES and Gender: Year 2

Grade	Total Group	A1 Boys	A1 Girls	B2 Boys	B2 Girls
1	72.7	56.0	67.0	83.9	72.0
2	84.4	75.0	82.5	85.5	86.0
3	77.5	73.0	67.3	82.3	79.0
4	73.5	73.0	60.0	81.0	81.0

A1 = Mother has high school   B2 = Mother has some
        education or less   college education

NOTE: Percentiles for disaggregated groups are for the mean raw scores for each group.

As indicated in Table 4.7, we note that apparently, even in the first grade, there was a difference on the California Achievement Test between girls and boys, but that difference for the lower socioeconomic group was reversed from the expected better performance by boys. The girls in the lower socioeconomic group did better on the test than the boys. Among the higher SES (B1) group, at the first grade, the boys outscored the girls, and both genders of the higher SES group outscored the lower SES (A1) group as predicted. The most interesting result in our disaggregation, however, was that the significant difference between the A1 boys and the B2 boys was somewhat overcome by the end of the fourth grade. A1 girls, on the other hand, lost ground, while the girls whose mothers had a college education caught up to their male counterparts at the same socioeconomic level.

Apparently, the new program worked really well at achieving equity for the A1 boys and B2 girls, but missed the A1 girls—with one exception. At the second-grade level, a group of experienced teachers, dedicated to the new approach, seemed to have achieved greater equity. It is my hypothesis that the "pictures in the heads," the motivating goals, of the A1 girls, which were placed there by mothers and teachers, were not easily overcome—except by particularly strong teaching. Gender, socioeconomic status, curriculum, and teaching are interactive variables. Disaggregation of scores can tell us what may need attention, and explain patterns of success and failure.

RELATIONSHIP OF TEACHER TRAINING AND EXPERIENCE TO STUDENT ACHIEVEMENT

One other school-based variable that we disaggregated for was the relationship between the overall test scores and two variables: the length of teachers'

Table 4.8

Teacher's Level of Experience and Training	Total Number of Teachers	Classes at or Above Mean on Both Tests	Classes at or Above Mean on One Test	Classes Below Mean on Both Tests
First year, no long-term training	9	0	4	5
First year plus long-term training	3	2	1	0
Second year plus long-term training	8	5	3	0

NOTE: All second-year teachers had taken the 25-hour, additional, formal-training component along with the three who participated before implementing the program. Chi-square analysis comparing this distribution of scores with expected distributions was significant at the .05 level, and Pearsons Product Moment of Correlation was significant at the .001 level.

experience with the reform program (we had piloted it at first) and voluntary engagement in a long term (25 hour), formal, professional-development program. Our analysis treated each variable separately and in combination. During the first piloting year, a voluntary, long-term, professional-development program was offered to all teachers in addition to the required training elements scheduled for all elementary participants. All the piloting teachers became involved as well as three non-piloting teachers.

Our analysis demonstrated that both the previous year's experience and the long-term, professional growth program made a difference, and in combination, they were the most effective. The group scores of more than half the classes of teachers who had 2 years experience and the formal professional development were above the district mean for both the CRT and the CAT. More than half of the classes of first-year teachers without formal professional development were below the mean for both tests (see Table 4.8).

OTHER CULTURAL AND SCHOOL VARIABLES: CONFRONTING THE ACHIEVEMENT GAP

Other cultural and school-based variables may have similar impact. The role of peers in influencing motivation and goals has been demonstrated as a strong possibility for creating and closing gaps. In a failing magnet school in Bath Beach, Brooklyn, a gifted program was added. It attracted neighborhood students who had previously traveled across the city to another place, leaving only the nonachievers behind. Within 5 years, the presence of the gifted students has turned the whole school around, and according to the principal, it is now a place where children come to learn instead of just to kill time (Biederman, 2001).

My current effort to help close the achievement gaps in the high-needs East Ramapo district addresses the need to raise another set of variables: student and teacher expectations. Although a Pearl River neighbor, East Ramapo is quite different in its larger size and diverse student population. We are engaging teachers in a program called Generating Expectations for Student Achievement (GESA), which was originally conceived and implemented in Los Angeles County by Dolores Grayson (Grayson & Martin, 2000). The program raises teachers' awareness of how they structure activities and provide feedback to their students. The premise on which it is based is that the perceptions and expectations of teachers, in their position of influence, can determine how their students act and affect student achievement, success, and productivity. GESA builds on what we have learned about the positive effects of self-efficacy, or the belief that one can accomplish a particular task, and the varying effects of culturally derived social goals (Solomon, 1998; Wentzel, 1993). It tries to change the "pictures in the heads" of students by helping teachers understand how to help the pictures change. Others can also help change the pictures.

In a personal interview just before he died, education's legendary Ralph Tyler stressed the importance of the school and family working together and reinforcing each other's goals (Horowitz, 1995). Commenting on the current National Association for the Advancement of Colored People (NAACP) agenda, noted journalist William Raspberry (2001) affirmed their focus on helping African American and Hispanic parents understand their critical importance in the academic success of their children:

> There are things parents can do both to show their children the long-term value of education and to help them acquire it—things like building self-discipline and self-respect, like practicing vocabulary and writing skills, like giving them affirming messages and tenderness. (p. 5B)

Some state governments are showing a little tenderness by slowing their timetables in response to negative reactions. In September 2001, the Arizona Department of Education suspended the Arizona Instrument for Measuring Standards (AIMS) test, giving high school students a break from the testing regimen. They also hired a new, private-testing contractor for $29 million over 5 years to retool the test and create new test questions (Flannery, 2001). Unfortunately, the vision of improved education through testing has not yet been realized for many minority students. Kati Haycock (2001), Director of The Education Trust, notes that although between 1970 and 1988 the gap between African American and white students was cut in half, since that time the gaps have widened, and she worries that educators have some wrong notions about the reasons for the slump. Haycock believes the solutions for closing the gap lie in standards and a challenging curriculum but cautions that students may need extra help within the school day and better teachers.

Teachers and principals can make a difference. Mosle (1996, pp. 41-45) tells the story of a Brooklyn, New York, principal who emphasized better scores on the standardized tests because they count. He has ninth graders take the SATs for fun and makes the test a positive cultural benchmark. Mosle, a former teacher in a different poorly achieving school in New York City, believes that a strong national curriculum and tests are the solution to the achievement gap. However, Father Matthew Foley, who leads a Brooklyn parish, believes that the negative home and community environment of many of the children who are not succeeding is too overwhelming. They need compensating opportunities to experience a different environment and develop better visions for their own futures. He offers some experimental proof for his ideas, which we will describe in our final chapter.

In order to improve schools, we must look at all the affecting variables, but to attain a positive effect, controlling those whose origins lie outside the school will prove to be the most difficult. Increasing our capacity to help our students learn by improving the connections and interactive responses between our curriculum and assessments may be the easier task. We will address these steps, including those in our East Ramapo effort, in the chapter ahead.

5 Responding to High-Stakes, Standards-Based (HSSB) Tests: Restructuring Curriculum

ABOUT THIS CHAPTER

Looking at the challenges of educational theory and practice for the 21st century, Schoenfeld (1999) reflects first on curriculum:

> Far too long there has been at best a tenuous relationship between curriculum development and research on thinking and learning. This has to change. If you really want kids to understand or do X, you need to know what it means to understand and do X. (p. 11)

He continues on assessment:

> You need to have an adequate characterization of what it is you're assessing, and you need to have a good idea of how performance on the assessment corresponds to being able to do whatever it is that's supposedly being assessed. (p. 11)

Schoenfeld proceeds to make change happen: "Sometimes you have to build something to see if it will work . . . and then you have to study the hell out of it" (p. 12).

The reality of what is happening at the beginning of the new century does not exactly follow Schoenfeld's sequence, but there has been a frenzy of experimental building. The underlying assumption for all of this building must be that it is possible for schools to do a better job of educating all students. This premise, however, does not necessarily agree with the evidence found by previous researchers. Much of the evidence gathered following the Coleman report (Hirsch, 1996) was not able to disprove Coleman's contention that it was only the home that created variations in student achievement. Given the same sociocultural environments, school-to-school differences could not be proven significant. Essentially stable scores over many years on national measures such as the National Assessment of Educational Progress affirmed the conclusion that there was little we could do by focusing on standards and improved curriculum.

International tests such as the Third International Math and Science Study (TIMSS), however, begin to give us some evidence that *what we do can matter.* In their analysis of the test results and curriculum across the diverse populations of different nations, Schmidt et al. (1999) discovered that differences are due to differences in what is taught. The very high performance of our student in science in the fourth grade is not maintained in the eighth grade and is way behind by the 12th grade: The authors also analyzed what the differences in curriculum and presentation are in such cases. They note, for example, that our curriculum is spread thin, with repetition but little depth. As we reported in Chapter 4, some of my own research over a long period of time, in a stable and homogeneous community, came to the same conclusion: Educators can make a difference.

This chapter comprises the plan for and implementation of immediate action to improve the curriculum and make that difference.

TWO ALTERNATIVE RESPONSES TO HSSB TESTS

We continue our bridge-building process with two alternative roadway structures of careful responses to the disaggregated analyses described in the previous chapter. The first alternative begins with the careful diagnoses of the embedded or underlying concepts of the HSSB test. These diagnoses are followed by examination of the existing curriculum to check that the concepts are there. Missing concepts need to be added. If they are present and the data reveal insufficient mastery, then better and appropriate learning experiences

Figure 5.1   A Design for Constructing Curriculum That Responds to HSSB Tests, With the Test at the Center

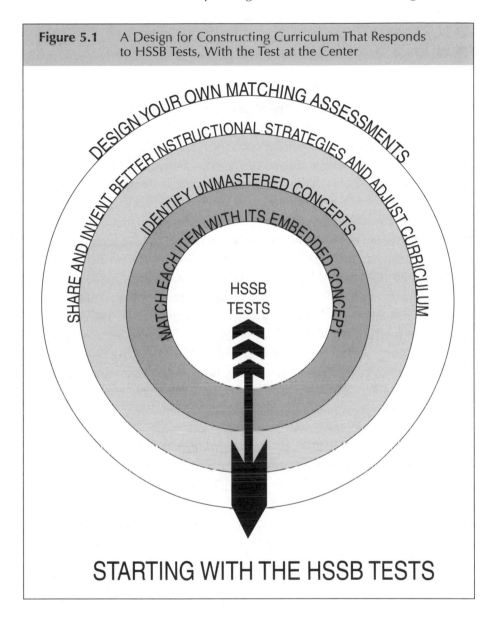

and resources are required. The final step might be to create matching, criterion-referenced, proximal assessments. As represented in Figure 5.1, this puts the HSSB test at the core (as the source of content standards) and works outward to the proximal matching assessments. Later, we will also offer an alternative, one that may be less immediately palliative but, in the long run, a better cure. Begin with the standards on which the test is based, design these down to the embedded concepts, match them to the HSSB tests, and then create your own formative and summative measure.

ALTERNATIVE ONE: STARTING WITH THE HSSB TEST

In the previous chapter, we mentioned Popham's (2001) distinction between *item teaching,* or practice with similar test items as preparation for a test, and *curriculum teaching,* which is directed at the content and skills represented by the test. A beginning step toward Popham's preferred latter approach is the identification of the content and skills embedded in each item. This concurs with Schoenfeld's (Schoenfeld, 1999) reflection that we need "an adequate characterization of what it is you're assessing" (p. 11). This is not an easy task; reaching consensus on what knowledge an assessment item requires is difficult.

Moss and Schutz (2001) question the "nature of the consensus reflected in educational standards used to orient high stakes assessment programs" (p. 37). They describe the give-and-take of extensive committee dialogues and reviews by stakeholders that preceded the publication of the written-standards documents produced by professional organizations. The documents themselves are finally published with disclaimers such as the one in the National Council of Teachers of Mathematics (NCTM) (2000) document that states that the standards "must periodically be examined, evaluated, tested by practitioners and revised" (p. x).

Considering the separate construction of assessment instruments, away from the original dialogue, Moss and Schutz wonder to what extent the standards are capable of supporting the decisions made as a result of performances on the assessments—decisions about student promotion, teacher tenure, and school funding. I share their doubts and, therefore, respond that in the directly affected community of decision makers about a particular HSSB test, there must be clarity and consensus on what students need to learn, and confidence that the given HSSB test provides unquestionable evidence that what was expected of the student, school, or teacher was or was not achieved.

The words themselves may have different meanings to different individuals. In her discussion of communication gaps in standards statements, Hill (2001) comments: "Words have no inherent meaning. Instead they signify ideas or actions ascribed to them by communities, and meanings vary across those communities" (p. 289). The term *embedded concepts* has appeared in this book as it applies to both curriculum and assessment items. In the community I wish to create with my readers, the embedded concepts are the specific vocabulary, facts, and relationships that the students must have in their long-term memory, which are required for a particular assessment item or for the mastery of a more general content standard.

EMBEDDED CONCEPTS

The term *embedded concepts* is used to differentiate a specific content standard from the more typical, general ones we find in most published documents. For example, a general social studies standard might be that students will know the causes of World War II. An embedded concept that may be required is that Germany and Japan had aggressively occupied the territory of other sovereign nations. A subconcept for the preceding concept may include representative names of some of the nations occupied. A related embedded concept might be that a sovereign nation is one whose government has sole ruling power over its inhabitants. Some might disagree with this defining concept, but it is important to reach some consensus on these embedded concepts for the purpose of assessment.

Although most states have made remarkable progress on the task of identifying standards, they have not, for the most part, reached the embedded-concept level. The American Federation of Teachers (AFT) (1999) in its study of state standards noted that although most of the states had developed standards, they did not satisfy teachers' requirements for clarity and specificity. It is interesting that the AFT also found them deficient in content (Section II, Major Findings, P1).

The first step toward successful systemic reform is to develop standards capable of supporting the reforms built around them. Many states, however, still do not have standards that satisfy our common core criterion's requirements for clarity, specificity, and being firmly grounded in content. And many states having generally strong standards still can benefit from some fine-tuning. Considering this need to rework the standards, it is encouraging to note that many states seem to view standards setting as a work in progress.

Admittedly, it may be impossible to uncover every required embedded concept, but the more explicitly these concepts are identified in the test items and stated in the curriculum, the greater the chances for student and teacher success. The assessment items in Figures 5.2A and 5.2B are from New York state's fourth- and eighth-grade math tests. Analysis of these items reveals that they assess a progression of embedded mathematical concepts, moving from an understanding of fractions and their application to a pie graph, to the ideas of certainty and uncertainty and the topic of probability.

A group of the possible probability concepts required for the preceding assessment items are presented in a tentative developmental sequence in Table 5.1. These concepts come from a published elementary middle-school set (Solomon, 2000) that I constructed from several curriculum sources and analyses, which were strengthened by interactive dialogue with teachers and students. They were designed down from more general content standards and performance indicators rather than from the items themselves. This group of concepts is not intended to incorporate every possible relationship or fact that is involved in solving the test items, and they do not describe additional, necessary process skills, such as estimation and problem solving. Nevertheless, they are an example of the kind of verbalizations of concepts

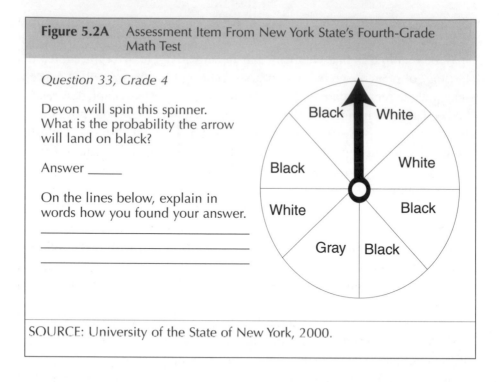

Figure 5.2A Assessment Item From New York State's Fourth-Grade Math Test

Question 33, Grade 4

Devon will spin this spinner. What is the probability the arrow will land on black?

Answer _____

On the lines below, explain in words how you found your answer.

_____
_____
_____

SOURCE: University of the State of New York, 2000.

that may help teachers and students understand what knowledge may be embedded in solutions for problems in probability. I actually used the whole set of concepts and performance indicators from which the Table 5.1 items are extracted as a supportive frame of reference with a group of teachers from several school districts as we tried to analyze the test items for their embedded concepts. Happily, the teachers added a few of their own. An added value of the identification of these concepts by teachers, as they review test items, is in the discourse with colleagues—much as the discourse I described from my own experience in Chapter 1. The outcome of such discourse is a comfortable consensus, which serves as a guide for adjusting curriculum, inventing new instructional strategies, and adding or correcting individual student knowledge.

ASSESSMENT-RESPONSIVE CURRICULUM ADJUSTMENTS

Identification of the embedded concepts is just the first step. As depicted in Figure 5.1, working outward from the core of tested concepts (or standards), those concepts that are not mastered and require attention must be identified or disaggregated. This needs to be followed by curriculum adjustments, the

Figure 5.2B   Assessment Item From New York State's Fourth-Grade
                   Math Test

Question 37, Grade 8

The Wheel of History game uses a
spinner divided into equal sections,
each labeled with a time period in
American history. A team member
spins the spinner and is asked a
question about the time period the
spinner lands on.

Part A

What is the probability that the
spinner will land on the time period
1800-1899?
Probability _____

Part B

The history department is planning to
write 60 questions for the game.
Based on the probability you gave in
Part A, how many questions should
be written for the period 1800-1899?
Answer _____

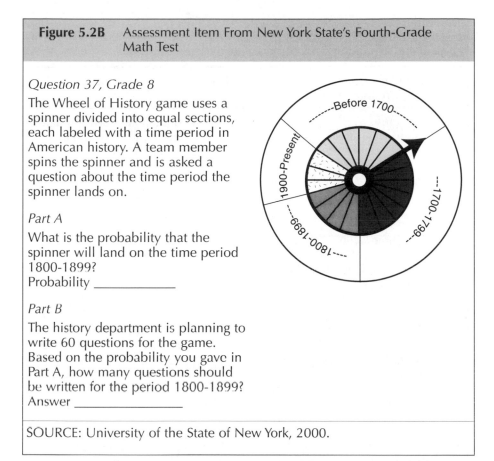

SOURCE: University of the State of New York, 2000.

invention of better instructional strategies, and the design of matching
proximal measures that can monitor ongoing progress.

STARTING FROM A CORE OF HSSB TESTS:
APPLYING AND RESPONDING TO ANALYSIS

Searching for an example of how this process can be played out, I recall a
very simple analysis and response. The analysis was initiated as I watched
fourth graders take a science performance assessment test in which they had
to measure a variety of items using instruments placed in front of them. I
noticed that although the students used their rulers and balances to measure
length and mass with ease, when confronted with measuring the volume of a
glass of water, they ignored a measuring cup and instead used their rulers to
record the height of the water in the glass.

    In my follow-up discussion with teachers, we identified the embedded
concepts as the knowledge that liquids take the shape of their container, and

Table 5.1   Embedded Concepts for Probability Questions

	Embedded Concepts (Content Standards)	Performance Indicators
73	Fractions can also be seen as patterns that help us compute totals. Five out of ten parts is the same as one out of two parts, or half the total number of parts.	Ability to **analyze word problems** and compute unknown quantities from the ratio pattern.
191	Sometimes, things are certain to occur, and other times, there is only a chance that they will happen.	Ability to distinguish between certain and chance events.
192	Outcomes are not always equally expected. For example, there is a greater chance of a warm day in July than in March—although it could happen.	Ability to identify factors that affect outcome of chance events. Ability to compute simple unequal-outcome probabilities.
193	Sometimes, we can predict the probability of uncertain events. If there are two choices on the spinner, we can predict that each choice will come up half the time. If there are more choices on the spinner, each choice will happen fewer times. If one die has only numbers 1, 2, 3 on it, and the other die has 1, 2, 3, 4, 5, 6, which one will show number 2 the most?	Ability to **compare probability of individual events given the number of choices**. Construction of a tree diagram or table of probable events.
194	We can prove our predictions by collecting data, but the data will not always be exact. The more data we collect, the closer to our prediction.	**Proof of inference** by collecting and collating data.

(continued)

Embedded Concepts (Content Standards)	Performance Indicators
195 Different objects can be combined into different groups or sets, but **a given number of objects can only be combined in a certain number of ways**. Tree diagrams and tables record combinations. You can make six different combinations of two objects out of four different objects if the way or order of how the objects are combined doesn't matter. For example, for objects R, W, Y, B; there can be RW, WY, YB, RB, WB, RY.	Ability to explain that objects can be differently arranged. Ability to compute number of sets of two from three or four different objects using real objects and tables. Ability to construct a tree diagram or table of possible events.
196 Sometimes the order does matter. Then there are more possibilities, because a switched order of the two objects makes a different case.	**Proof of inference** using tree diagrams as real data.
197 As the number of objects combined into one group increases, the number of possibilities changes.	Construction of a tree diagram or table of possible events. **Generalizations about the relationships between number of objects in a group and possibilities**.

SOURCE: Adapted from Solomon (2000).

that, therefore, they can only be measured by placing them into a standard instrument—a measuring cup or graduated cylinder. The performance indicator would be their ability to correctly use the standard. We agreed that these concepts were missing from our curriculum and activities. I wondered why and discovered that teachers were not as open to measuring liquids in the classroom because of the mess created. I also reflected on the fact that my own informal experiences were full of the need to use standard measures. But these suburban children were not the children of rural farmers or storekeepers, and even recipes made from scratch are rarely seen by children at home in our current culture. We quickly remedied this deficiency by adding liquid measuring experiences in classrooms.

As we examine most of the standards documents issued by professional organizations and state education departments, we discover some excellent beginnings in the statements of performance indicators, but they are only beginnings. In contrast to the specific embedded concepts presented in Table 5.1, most state standards documents are more general and tend to include just the skill-based performance indicators. In an intensive professional-development institute in the summer of 2000, I worked with a multidistrict group of teachers to analyze the mathematics test questions. We were helped with a published list of embedded concepts (Solomon, 2000) but added additional ones. In addition to the identified concepts, we added suggestions for possible resources to help improve understanding.

An interesting component of this institute was the presence of teachers at grade levels that preceded the testing level. They identified embedded concepts that would be appropriate for their level as well as resources. This was an important breakthrough in that it relieved teachers at the tested grade of complete responsibility for concepts that need to be developed over time. The sharing of responsibility for test preparation by all teachers can relieve some of the pressure on teachers and students at the tested grade levels. K-12 connections are critical because "it is important for teachers to know how what they do now with children bears on later learning" (de Groot, 2000, p. 23). It may take more effort to develop a concept with meaning than to teach a simple procedure by rote, but the concept has longevity and breadth that will make it much more valuable in the future. Increased teacher knowledge of the concepts required can be incorporated into proximal tests at every grade, and student deficiencies can be diagnosed and remedied before the testing year. For example, for question 33 of the fourth-grade test (Figure 5.2A), a second-grade teacher identified applicable concepts for her students (Table 5.2).

ALTERNATIVE TWO: STARTING WITH THE STANDARDS

Given the choice in a period of less exigency, I would begin my approach to school improvement by rebuilding the curriculum, with constant attention to the relationship between the whole and parts, embedded concepts, and matching performance measures. The whole of the curriculum is the consensus of the culture. It is what the stakeholders want their students to have at the end. In standards language, this consensus would comprise the commencement-level content standards. Most standards documents begin this way, with very general all-inclusive statements. Commencement-level standards are then also sometimes designed down to equally general benchmarks, which describe progress toward the commencement standard at the different levels. Benchmarks frame the larger parts. These then have to be designed down into the smaller parts of more specific embedded concepts and skills.

Teachers always dealt with the small parts in their day-to-day lessons but rarely looked back at the whole to ask the following questions:

> How does this lesson prepare my students for more complex knowledge in the future?

Table 5.2   Concepts for Second Graders, Based on Question 33 for Fourth
                  Graders

Number	Embedded Concepts (Content Standard)	Performance Indicators
62	Whole things can be equally shared. The whole then becomes parts with special names depending on their size. These parts are named fractions.	Ability to identify one-half of a whole item in a word problem picture.
63	The more parts made out of a whole, the smaller the part. The bottom number of the fraction (denominator) tells you how many parts were made from the whole. The top number (numerator) tells you how many of these parts you are thinking about.	Ability to predict the size of a part compared to another when the number of sharers is known, and recognize the number of parts the whole has been divided into from the fraction name.
191	Sometimes, things are certain to occur, and other times, there is only a chance that they will happen.	Ability to distinguish between certain and chance events.
192	Outcomes are not always equally expected. For example, there is a greater chance of a warm day in July than in March—although it could happen.	Ability to identify factors that affect outcome of chance events. Ability to compute simple, unequal-outcome probabilities.

SOURCE: Solomon (2000).

How can this new concept be generalized into a larger theme or big idea?

How can I make connections between what students are learning here and now and prior knowledge constructed in school or informally?

How can I prepare them to reconstruct this knowledge if they perceive new data?

Active participation and interaction with colleagues in the design-down process may help teachers and their students make the upward and sideward connections as well. Nevertheless, identifying the concepts is still only part of the way. The process for helping students construct the concepts requires carefully orchestrated learning experiences and supportive materials.

As any teacher knows, when learning how to perform a complex process, it is wise to begin with a less-complex small sample. It is also wise to begin with something familiar. Designing a whole curriculum down from the commencement standards to individual lessons is a monumental task. It may be better to begin with a familiar 2-week unit. In a 1998 intensive institute at St. Thomas Aquinas College for 130 teachers from eight very different school districts, I led teams of teachers through the process of designing curriculum down from the general state standards toward more specific, embedded concepts. Their designs were integrated into 2-week curriculum units that they could use in their own classrooms.

The teachers came in pairs from individual schools as what we called PIPs, or peer interactive partners, but were then combined into interdistrict working groups. College faculty members from a variety of subject areas were also engaged with the secondary school teacher groups, and teacher-educators worked with the elementary teachers. The college faculty designed their own curriculum units and also served as a resource for the working groups. In addition to the subject area standards, each unit was engineered to include technology applications. Small-group meetings in the fall followed an intensive few days in the summer. The idea was to pilot the curriculum as it was developed and share results with colleagues. It was at the small-group meetings that the important consensus-building process of identifying embedded concepts was realized. It was difficult to select samples, because they are all very good. The specificity and creativity of the rubrics are indications that the informal assessments of this teacher group are very effective.

A large group of the units that range from kindergarten to college level, which teachers allowed to be shared, may be individually accessed at the St. Thomas Aquinas College Marie Curie Center Web site from a list of curriculum designs found at the site (www.stac.edu/mcc/indexrev.htm). The units themselves were truly wonderful and have been shared over our Web site with many others. There readers will discover a range of units covering first grade to upper-level college biochemistry. Readers can look for the "Index to Designs" at the site and find a particular unit of curriculum matched to the grade level and the typical, more general state standards.

The template in Table 5.3 was the shared structure for all units; and the rubric in Table 5.4 was used to evaluate each unit and provide guidance for better detail. This template has subsequently been productively used by many students, teachers, and schools as a model for designing curriculum matched to state standards.

We have chosen some excerpts from these units to illustrate particular functions and applications. Table 5.5 is adapted from a unit by teacher Andrea L. Holland to show how the template design based on Table 5.3 can be applied. Readers should note how the more general state standards are then designed down to benchmarks and individual unit concepts. They might also note how the sample activity (one of several in the full unit) matches the

Table 5.3   Template for Curriculum Design

The subject and grade level that this unit aims for:
The in-school time total for this unit:
The theme or topic of this unit:

✓ **Commencement content standard(s):**
Choose those that are applicable to this unit from state or district standards
(*what students should know and be able to do when they graduate*).

✓ **Benchmark content standards:** Choose the designed-down content standards
at your benchmark (elementary, intermediate, senior high school, or college)
that this unit aims for. Benchmark standards may be those for the next-higher
level at which there is a state assessment.

✓ **Content standards and performance indicators for your unit:** Identify all the
specific concepts and skills you will be assessing. These should help your
students meet the standards.

    A. Content standards: What you want your students to know
    B. Performance indicators: What you want your students to be able to do

✓ **Assessment rubric:** Describe the rubric you will be using to define levels of
performance. Use four progressive levels and be as specific as possible. The
standard level of the rubric should define the performance standard or "how
good is good enough."

✓ **Enactment activities:** Describe the activities in which you will engage your
students over the total unit length of time. Estimate the time for each activity.

standard. The entire unit may be accessed at www.stac.edu/mcc/holland
(retrieved from the Web, January 30, 2002).

The evaluation rubric by teachers Pam Deming and Eva Simon in
Table 5.6 allows second-grade students to self-assess their computer-
generated presentations on dinosaurs. Readers should note the clarity of the
expectations for process and content that are shared with the student ahead
of time. The entire unit may be accessed at www.stac.edu/mcc/deming
(retrieved from the Web, January 30, 2002).

(text continues on page 97)

Table 5.4   Rubric for Evaluating Standards-Based Curriculum

Check the appropriate description.

Level 4: Above Standard

☐ State standards clearly defined as content standards and performance standards.

☐ Designed-down unit standards articulated with state commencement standards and show clear and appropriate developmental levels toward reaching them.

☐ Unit enactment activities articulated to accomplish standards and inspire students to go beyond the standards.

☐ Performance measures designed to diagnose deficiencies in standards achievement and direct students and teachers toward remediation measures.

☐ Activities clearly outlined, creative, and inspiring for others to follow.

☐ Technology creatively employed.

Level 3: At Standard

☐ State standards clearly defined as content standards and performance standards.

☐ Designed-down unit standards appropriately articulated with state commencement and benchmark standards.

☐ Unit enactment activities articulated to accomplish standards.

☐ Performance measures adequately measure standards.

☐ Activities clearly outlined for others to follow. Activities original or appropriate adaptations.

☐ Technology employed.

Level 2: Approaching Standard

☐ State standards clearly defined as content standards and performance standards.

☐ Some designed-down unit standards not appropriately articulated with state commencement and benchmark standards.

☐ Some unit enactment activities not articulated well enough to accomplish standards.

☐ Performance measures not articulated well enough to adequately measure standards.

☐ Some activities not clearly enough outlined for others to follow. Some originality.

☐ Technology not adequately employed.

Level 1: Below Standard

☐ State standards not clearly defined as content standards and performance standards.

☐ Designed-down unit standards not appropriately articulated with state commencement and benchmark standards.

☐ Unit enabling activities not articulated well enough to accomplish standards.

☐ Performance measures not articulated well enough to adequately measure standards.

☐ Enabling activities not clearly enough outlined for others to follow. Little originality.

☐ Technology not applied.

Table 5.5 Curriculum Design Example

✓ Commencement content standard(s):
What students should know and be able to do when they graduate

The subject and grade level that this unit aims for: Mathematics Grade 2
The in-school time total for this unit: 2 weeks
The theme or topic of this unit: addition, operations, and patterns

New York State Standard 3: Mathematics, Science, and Technology: Students will understand mathematics and become mathematically confident by communicating and reasoning mathematically; by applying mathematics to real-world settings; and by solving problems through the integrated study of number systems, geometry, algebra, data analysis, probability, and trigonometry.

✓ Benchmark content standards: Elementary

Number and Numeration: Students use number sense and numeration to develop an understanding of multiple uses of numbers in the real world, use of numbers to communicate mathematically, and use of numbers in the development of mathematical ideas.

Operations: Students use mathematical operations and relationships among them to understand mathematics.

Patterns: Students use patterns and functions to develop mathematical power, appreciate the true beauty of mathematics, and construct generalizations that describe patterns simply and efficiently.

✓ Content standards and performance indicators

The children will

- Recognize that the addition process is combining parts to make a whole
- Use the symbol + to represent the combination of two parts to make a whole
- Create, extend, and identify 2-part patterns using a variety of materials
- Use manipulatives to explore number sentences, operations, and their relationship, and the commutative property of addition
- Be able to divide groups of objects into equal parts
- Successfully add and subtract using 1-digit numbers

(continued)

Table 5.5 Continued

✓ **Assessment Rubric:** Describe the rubric you will be using to define levels of performance. Use four progressive levels and be as specific as possible. The standard level of the rubric should define the performance standard or "how good is good enough."

Criteria for scoring skills are listed below:

4 = Application Mastery (can generate an original problem using the concept and apply it)

3 = Procedural Mastery (can generalize the concept and use it to solve problems without manipulatives)

2 = Concept Mastery (can solve problems and explain the concept used, with or without manipulatives)

1 = Procedural Exploration (can solve problems based on the concept using real and concrete representative materials)

Content Skills	**Data Collection Skills**	**Dispositions and Interactions**
• Can do one-to-one count to 20 • Knows ordinal numbers to tenth • Can skip count by 2, 3, 4, 5, 10 • Recognizes pattern in math equations • Uses and creates number sentences • Recognizes and demonstrates commutative properties of addition • Recognizes and demonstrates associative property of addition • Follows auditory and visual patterns	• Journal exhibits skills. • Journal is neat and readable. • Journal follows correct format including date on each page. • Numbers are written correctly. • Journal shows growth in performance and knowledge. • Representations of two-part patterns are correctly drawn. • Journal is completed with accuracy. • Work is completed neatly.	• Demonstrates confidence in skill • Demonstrates skills to others • Discusses importance of patterns in math

Enactment Activities: Describe the activities in which you will engage your students over the total unit length of time. Estimate the time for each activity.

Symbolic representation of a two-part pattern.   Time: 50 minutes

Materials: journal; 20 cubes, 10 of one color, 10 of a second color (in a baggy); strips of paper with equally spaced dots; pencil and crayons

Introduction: Organize children into pairs. Review two-part pattern using both colors and sounds.

Body: Instruct children to create their own two-part patterns. Introduce the strips with the dots. Ask how the children think they can create a pattern using the dot strip. Introduce the bump and straight vocabulary. Encourage children to model with their body what a bump might look like and what straight might look like. Model this using the dot strip. While working in pairs, have the children create patterns using bump and straight. Encourage the creation of any symbols that might also be appropriate.

Questions: What do you think a bump looks like? What do you think straight looks like? Can you show me? Can you think of some other symbols we can use on the dot strip? What do you think we can use these dot strips for? Can you make a pattern using the dot strip? Can you show me the bump and straight pattern using your body?

Literature Link: *Seven Blind Mice* by Ed Young

Follow-up Activity: Paste the strip to the journal and have all the children model their pattern with their bodies. Using Microsoft Word, the children can create bump and straight patterns using the insert lines and freeform line functions.

Conclusion: All the children have the opportunity to demonstrate to the class their bump and straight patterns. Patterns may include other activities and may become three or four part. Materials are returned to appropriate place and cubes are returned to the baggy.

SOURCE: Adapted with permission from Andrea L. Holland. May be retrieved at www.stac.edu/mcc/holland.htm (retrieved from the Web, January 30, 2002).

Table 5.7, written by teacher Patricia De Noble, presents a Grade 3 social studies curriculum unit based on the template in Table 5.3. Readers should note the design-down increase in specificity from the very general commencement level to the most specific rubric, and then the hearkening back to the commencement standard in the sample activity. Readers may also note the application of technology, and the progression from flat map to globe to the virtual applications of the Internet.

Although the general state standards had been issued at the time we completed the curriculum work described above, the whole assessment package was not yet in place, and tensions were not as high. Three years later, the tone of the times was quite different, but schools and teachers may still find it more meaningful to start with the standards, design them down to the more specific embedded concepts, compare them to the HSSB tests, searching for needed revisions, and then design their own proximal assessment to match. This is the process we employed in response to test data that diagnosed the need for improvement as described below.

(text continues on page 102)

Table 5.6   Self-Assessment for Dinosaur Project

Culminating Assessment: As a final project, each student will be asked to do research on a dinosaur of choice. The student must answer the following questions:

During which period did your dinosaur live?
What does its name mean?
What did it eat?
What was its length?
Where have its bones been found?
What other facts have you learned about this dinosaur?

Children will be given a choice, if available, of using HyperStudio or PowerPoint as a method of presenting their research information to the class. If a scanner is available, children will be required to find a picture of their dinosaur and include it in the presentation. This project will be assessed using the Grade-2 Dinosaur Project Rubric, which the children will be given in advance.

Grade-2 Dinosaur Project Rubric

	4	3	2	1
Knowledge Learned	I answered all six of the questions completely.	I answered five of the six questions completely.	I answered four of the six questions completely.	I answered three or fewer of the questions completely.
Technological Presentation	I used at least four slides. I used graphics and fade-outs.	I used fewer than four slides. I used graphics and fade-outs.	I did not use slides, or I did not use graphics and fade-outs.	I did not use slides, and I did not use graphics and fade-outs.
Oral Presentation	I spoke in a clear, loud voice. I shared my facts and answered questions.	My voice was loud and clear most of the time. I shared my facts and answered most questions.	My voice was NOT loud and clear. I did NOT share my facts. I answered some questions.	My voice was NOT loud and clear. I did NOT share my facts. I did NOT answer questions.

SOURCE: Adapted with permission from a curriculum unit by teachers Pam Deming and Eva Simons.

Table 5.7   Curriculum Design Example

✓ Commencement Content Standard(s):
What students should know and be able to do when they graduate

New York State Social Studies Standards
- Standard 7: All students will acquire geographical understanding by studying spatial terms.
- Standard 8: All students will acquire geographical understanding by studying human systems in geography.

✓ Elementary Benchmark-Level Performance Indicators

Students will be able to

- Use maps, globes, graphs, diagrams, and computer-based references and information to generate and interpret information
- Use mental maps to identify the locations of places within the local community and nearby communities
- Use mental maps to identify the locations of the earth's continents and oceans in relation to each other
- Use mental maps to identify the locations of major physical and human characteristics in the United States
- Demonstrate understanding of the spatial concepts of location, distance, direction, scale, region, and movement

✓ Unit Content Standards and Performance Indicators
- **Content standards (what you want your students to know)**
- **Performance indicators (what you want your students to be able to do)**

Students will be able to
- Describe how to get from one location to another in their school and classroom
- Identify related locations by familiar landmarks, e.g., school, stores, or parks
- Locate and identify land and water forms on a map or a globe
- Identify the cardinal directions of north, east, south, and west
- Verbally explain and understand the relationships to function and spatial location that are present among their neighbors and community helpers
- Locate or move from one location to another on a map or globe
- Identify and use the terms up, down, left, right, backward, straight, and forward

✓ Assessment Rubric

Level 1: Below Level

- Students cannot identify and use the cardinal directions (east, north, south, and west).
- Students are unable to distinguish and identify the terms up, down, left, right, backward, straight, and forward to find their present location.

(continued)

Table 5.7 Continued

- Students cannot use the cardinal directions (east, north, south, and west) or the indicated terms to find their location on a map or globe.
- Students are unable to clearly explain verbally the relationship that is present among their neighbors and community helpers.
- Students cannot distinguish between land and water forms on a map or globe.

Level 2: Approaching Standard

- Students can identify and use some of the cardinal directions (east, north, south, and west).
- Students are able to define and apply some of the terms up, down, left, right, backward, straight, and forward to find their present location.
- Students are capable of using the cardinal directions and indicated terms to find some locations on a map or globe.
- Students are able to verbally explain some relationships that are present among their neighbors and community helpers.
- Students can identify some land and water forms on a map and on a globe.

Level 3: At Standard

- Students are able to clearly identify and use all the cardinal directions (east, north, south, and west).
- Students can define and apply all the terms up, down, left, right, backward, straight, and forward to find their present location.
- Students are able to use all the cardinal directions and indicated terms to find their location on a map or a globe.
- Students are able to clearly define the relationships to function and spatial location that are present among their neighbors and community helpers.
- Students can accurately distinguish between land and water forms on a map and a globe.

Level 4: Above Standard

- Students grasp and understand the cardinal directions and use all the indicated terms to find various locations outside the classroom and within the school environment.
- Students are able to recognize and explain the similarities and differences between representations on a map and a globe.
- Students can describe the relationships to function and spatial location among their neighbors and community helpers with specific references.

ENACTMENT ACTIVITIES

Lesson Four: This activity addresses commencement standard #7.

Materials: Globe, flat map

Procedure:

Introduce to the students both the globe and the flat map.

1. Ask the students:

   - What are the *differences* between the globe and a map? (One is round and one is flat.)
   - What are the *similarities* between the globe and a map? (They both have oceans and land.)
   - Do they both use the directions north, south, east, and west? Can you identify and point to the water on the map and then on the globe? Can you identify and point to the land on the map and then on the globe?
   - Are these the same or different on the map and globe?

2. Divide the class into cooperative learning groups. Give one group a flat map and the other group a globe to look at.

   - Group one will be given the task to list why it is better to use a globe. (Provide a globe for this group to examine.)
   - Group two will be given the task to list why it is better to use a map. (Provide maps for this group to look at.)

3. Allow the students time to discuss and construct their responses to the assignment. Then regroup and discuss the groups' answers.

Lesson 10: This activity addresses commencement standards #7 and #8.

Materials: Computer and Internet access

Procedure:

To conclude and review the concepts of the unit study on map and spatial terms, log on to www.nationalgeographic.com/maps/* This will allow students to view the various types of maps available through the Internet. It will also familiarize the students with using the computer as a valuable resource. Model an example for the students to see before asking them any questions concerning the activity.

1. Ask the students: How can the Internet help us find our location? Can the Internet help find the directions to some place that we need to go? How is finding our location on the Internet different from using a map to find a location? How is using the Internet the same as using a map?

2. Then allow small groups of students to use the computers to find map directions from their homes to the school. Give the students the school address to aid in their search. After the students have completed this task, allow them to print out the directions.

3. Once the students have their map directions printed out, have them circle the terms north, south, east, west, right, left, straight, up, and down. These are all terms that the students have been introduced to during the 2-week unit.

   (*Retrieved January 24, 2002, from the Internet.)

SOURCE: Adapted from a Grade-3 curriculum unit by teacher Patricia deNoble. Used with permission.

RESPONDING TO TEST DATA
WITH CURRICULUM RECONSTRUCTION

Starting in the spring of 2001, as part of a professional development school relationship between St. Thomas Aquinas College and the East Ramapo schools, a large and diverse school district, we approached the task of improving student achievement in a holistic and comprehensive fashion. Scores on the state assessments were not good when compared with neighboring districts. The educators could have placed the blame on student diversity and the lower socioeconomic status of the district, but their response was quite different. They recognized that there was a critical need to reorganize the upper elementary and middle school math and science curriculum so there would be better articulation between the programs and a gradual development of skills. This was ostensibly a crisis management approach, but one focused on curriculum teaching rather than on item teaching (teaching to the test). It is essentially based on the assumption that state HSSB tests are based on the state standards and that if we incorporate the standards into our curriculum and monitor our students' progress, we are preparing them for the distal tests.

Ownership for the curriculum-teaching approach is immediate and less tense because the source of the specifics are proximal, and there is greater control over the whole. In East Ramapo, both science and math teacher planning groups selected some more familiar theme units and connected them first to the more general state standards' and then to more specific, designed-down, embedded concepts. The science planning group recognized that an understanding of the role of inquiry in science, and student materials for inquiry, experiences were a major priority. They therefore decided to pilot different commercial kits of science materials and evaluate them in terms of their ability to help students achieve the chosen concepts. For math, plans are in process to share and then incorporate teachers' suggestions for classroom strategies and materials as they progress through the new curriculum. The final phase for both the math and science groups will be the construction of matching performance indicators with their own assessments.

Our work with early literacy was also an example of alternative two, curriculum teaching, but slightly different, because the emphasis was on a set of specific skills rather than on a combination of concepts and skills organized into a curriculum unit. The early literacy planning group decided that what was needed was professional development designed to help teachers identify, assess, and provide learning experiences for a carefully sequenced set of early literacy skills.

The sequence for the alternative of starting with the standards, designing them down to their clearly identified embedded concepts and skills (curriculum teaching), and matching these with performance indicators and proximal assessments is depicted in Figure 5.3.

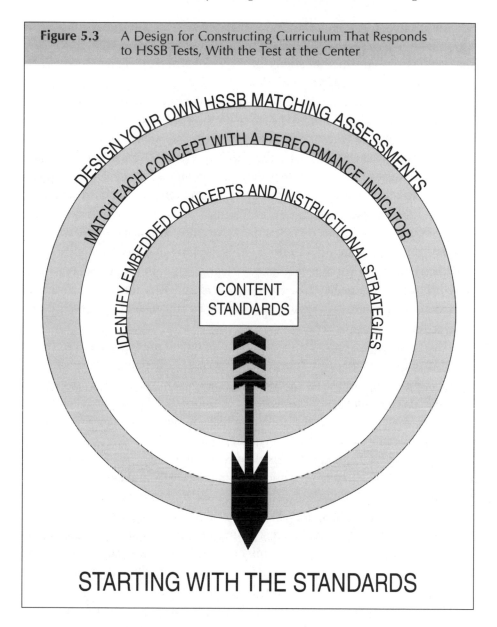

Figure 5.3 A Design for Constructing Curriculum That Responds to HSSB Tests, With the Test at the Center

DESIGN YOUR OWN HSSB MATCHING ASSESSMENTS

MATCH EACH CONCEPT WITH A PERFORMANCE INDICATOR

IDENTIFY EMBEDDED CONCEPTS AND INSTRUCTIONAL STRATEGIES

CONTENT STANDARDS

STARTING WITH THE STANDARDS

IN CONCLUSION: ASSESSING ONESELF

Standards may be defined, interpreted, applied, and measured in many different, but often overlapping, ways. It may be important to remember, however, that there is a strong human imperative to judge oneself. Standards may be the performer's own and the measure may be of self-evaluation. Infants takes great pleasure in their first successful attempt to reach for something or stand, not because they measure themselves against an external standard but because they have a strong human need to have power over the environment in which they find themselves. Our ability to control the environment is an internal standard that is with us always. Although we may make revisions and modifications in response to other goals, we measure ourselves against this standard until we die.

The common connotation for performance standards is that they are externally imposed measures. This may be the case if we don't create environments in which teachers and students are motivated to set their own performance standards and take their own measures—or at least measure themselves against a standard that they understand and accept. Undeniably, we live in a social world and, therefore, respect externally imposed standards because they represent the consensual domain of knowledge and skills. The revisions we make in our own standards are most often based on what we observe that others are able to do and on the judgments of others. Schools and their students owe their audiences clearly communicated evidence that they are meeting expectations. However, it is our own constant measure of how we ourselves are progressing that directs us and drives us over a lifetime to ever-higher levels of achievement.

Unfortunately, educators' measures of students' progress are not always so clear-cut, and more often than not, they do not challenge us or our students to try harder or motivate us to find out exactly why we were unsuccessful. Although we constantly assess students in informal ways as we teach them, we rarely openly attribute the student's lack of success to our own performance. How rarely are we apt to say, "I am sorry that you didn't understand. Perhaps I didn't do a good job of explaining what was needed"? And we often do not engage and encourage students to methodically and consciously evaluate themselves. Modeling of self-assessment by teachers and more structured opportunities for self-evaluation by students might be helpful. The standards or levels of the bar against which we most frequently measure ourselves in schools are socially determined. And though we usually accept the results as personal, these measured demonstrations are often designed for the benefit of another audience and for different purposes.

It is important to understand the different purposes of measured demonstrations or assessments, because although they may overlap, different purposes require different measures.

Parents and the public have an important investment in the education of our students. They are a critical and demanding audience. On a broader scale, the public audience demands accountability for the dollars spent on education and attributes socioeconomic problems to school failure. HSSB assessments are meaningful to this audience because they believe that the tests are controlled, reliable, and valid. Although only broadly assessing the child's individual progress and rarely diagnosing specific needs, HSSB tests do provide comparison to a norm and allow parents and others to evaluate children and their schools in relation to others. Educated parents recognize the highly competitive culture in which we live and worry about their offspring's chances for success.

Better proximal assessments of individual progress, matched to embedded concepts and clarified with shared rubrics in the curriculum, might be able to sway parents from preoccupation with these incompletely revealing HSSB measures. The tests may also have greater meaning for the many uninformed parents who do not understand standardized and normed tests and may consider them unfair and biased for children whose cultures are different from the norming sample. Although the purpose of HSSB assessment is to evaluate the system rather than the individual child, we can construct our assessment bridge by connecting this purpose to our own purposes with a solid roadway of matching curriculum with our own measures. We need some help. The remaining chapters will address the need for greater teacher capacity and leadership.

6 Building a Cohort of the Best Teachers: Recruitment, Engagement, Nurturance

ABOUT THIS CHAPTER

I have been most fortunate in my long career as an educator to have had so many opportunities to work directly with young people. Even as a college professor, I designed and managed the Saturday morning program for 5th- to 12th-grade students that I described in Chapter 3. I learned so much from listening to them and watching them learn. Most fortunately, I can still listen and learn because a new and different opportunity has arisen for me these past few years. I have become a car pool grandma, bringing my own two grandchildren and various friends home from school each day. In the car, I do not seem to exist. Conversations overheard are the conversations usually reserved for sharing only among the young. I try not to interject, because I want to listen.

Teachers are sometimes the topic, and the evaluations are rarely positive. I was, therefore, quite surprised today with the conversation and with a response to my question from 13-year-old Joseph. He had proudly boasted to his friends about his A on a math test, and I couldn't resist asking the question, "How come you are suddenly doing so well in math, when I rarely see you doing math homework?" Without hesitation he replied, "I have a new, really good teacher and learn in school. I don't need a lot of homework to do well on the test." It was a reassuring comment that supported my strong belief that good teaching can make a difference. It may not be able to get every child to the same level, but good teaching can make every child grow and want to grow more.

Good teachers are a critical component of the solution to our current problems. The major difficulty today is finding good teachers, keeping them, and helping them continue to grow. It is customary for engineers, before they begin actual construction of a bridge, to test their ideas with a model. This chapter presents a model for building a cohort of the best teachers.

ABOUT MODELS

There are many kinds of models. System models can help us understand and predict how things work or can break down. They provide us with patterns to follow or to use as a framework for our own innovations. Human beings have used them well. We have even used the special characteristics of plants and animals to help us. Medieval armor imitated the protective shells of turtles and some invertebrates. Our first attempts to fly were patterned after the birds, and the camouflage of a soldier's uniform comes from imitation of the protective coloration of successful organisms.

There are also human models. I was rather shocked the other day by a newscast interview of an Arab mother whose son died in a terrorist attack. Her fondest wish, she proclaimed, was that her other son would die in the same way. Human models play an important role in society, especially when they are considered heroes. Instead of haphazard attempts to deal with our current educational problems, it may be wise to examine models that are successful—even models from the past. We also need to find and celebrate worthy human heroes. I do have a model in mind for meeting the demands of the new millennium for a highly qualified and multiculturally representative pool of teachers and keeping them. The model focuses on three aspects of the challenges faced in doing this: *recruitment, engagement,* and *nurturance* (REN).

WHY WE NEED TO RECRUIT TEACHERS

The need for attracting qualified new entrants into a career that has little of the glamour and few of the financial awards that seem to attract young people to other careers at the beginning of the 21st century is well documented and universal in the United States. In a revealing national study, Ingersoll (1999) found strikingly high percentages of public secondary positions filled with teachers working without certification and a correspondingly high number teaching a subject for which they did not have a major. Underqualified teachers were present in a wide range of fields such as mathematics, science, English, and history.

Under pressure to staff classrooms, states have responded and are making unprecedented attempts to deal with the problem. Sometimes, the obstacle is not the number of teacher candidates but their ability to demonstrate minimal competency requirements. The Illinois state teacher certification board created a more difficult certification test but then lowered the passing rate in an effort to help struggling teachers pass the tests. Even with a lowered passing score, only 76% of those who took the test passed. The passing rate for minority candidates was particularly disappointing in light of the desire to appoint more teachers from this group (Rossi, 2001). On the other hand, Utah is bending with the wind by making teacher certification available through Internet courses and giving credit for "competency-based accreditation" (Weiner, 2001).

In New York City, uncertified teachers fill as many as 50% of secondary science, special education, and foreign language positions. In the fall of 2000, the city brought 53 teachers from Austria to fill the vacant spots. For 2001, the expectation for foreign recruitment in New York City is about 800. Los Angeles, Chicago, and Houston are also expecting to recruit an average of about 90 foreign teachers in 2001 (Goodnough, 2001b). Even the suburban schools complain about the lack of high-quality teaching candidates for some positions. They steal strong candidates from the city schools and from each other. To avoid the anxiety of unexpected, last-minute empty classrooms, our local county administrators finally signed a written agreement not to hire an incumbent teacher from another district in the county after a certain date.

The immediacy of the need for teachers may require consideration of a variety of alternative certification programs including distance-learning technology and for-profit alternatives. Zeichner and Schulte (2001) suggest that instead of seeking to determine which method of attaining certification is best, we use our energy to ensure the uniformity of high quality for each possible form. They further recommend that we pay attention to the salaries and working conditions of those already hired so that we do not lose them. We also need to understand why the shortage developed in the first place.

The cause of this shortage is a combination of factors that differentially affect original recruitment and retention. The original recruitment deficit is most certainly affected by competition from other, more lucrative and prestigious careers and a simultaneous loss of prestige for the teaching profession. Retention of teachers is, no doubt, affected by working conditions and the possibilities of early retirement, which in some cases has been encouraged. The unfortunate result is a diminution of quality in those who teach.

WHERE TEACHERS USED TO COME FROM

In the 19th century, most teachers and the staffs of the normal schools that trained them were female. It was one of the very few choices for educated and mostly unmarried women. As I reflect on the time of my entry into the profession, I recall that it was a preferred choice for my female counterparts. Being a Phi Beta Kappa mathematics or chemistry major did not ensure entry into a male-dominated and narrow field of positions for people with such skills. Besides, the culture of the time put a premium on family. Teaching offered some compromises: a job near home, in-school hours that coincided with your children's hours (teachers could do lesson planning and paper grading at night or in the early morning before their children were awake), summer vacations, liberal maternity leaves (I took a total of 8 years for two children), security, and the opportunity to learn and grow.

We also had a wonderful set of teacher role models, both male and female, who entered the profession during the depression years when the security and prestige of being a teacher lured a force of enthusiastic, bright people, many of whom were the highly educated children of immigrants. Although there was also a cadre of male secondary school entrants into the profession from the group of returning World War II veterans, most of the post–Depression era men preferred the more competitive professions. Another spate of very successful male teachers came in the 1960s when a teaching position exempted one from being drafted for service in the Vietnam War. Many of these men later became school administrators.

WHY THERE IS A CURRENT SHORTAGE: THE RECRUITMENT POOL

As the role of women in the culture changed and previously limited opportunities opened up to them, fewer of the top male or female college students made the choice to teach. How could a beginning teaching job, which required a master's degree within 5 years and paid $30,000 with only the promise of small, yearly, union-prescribed increments, compare with a beginning salary of $90,000—with the added prospect of bonuses and rapid advancement—on Wall Street or in Silicon Valley?

It is only very recently that I see a small blip of young men and women who, having been turned off by the pace and cutthroat environment of our modern economy, reconsider teaching as a profession that provides better opportunities for security, personal growth, and fulfilling human relationships.

They are, for the most part, mature and capable individuals who offer fine prospects for the future of the profession. Unfortunately, the second-career group and the small number of undergraduates prepared to teach is not nearly large enough to replace the large numbers of retiring teachers and meet the demand by increasing numbers of students. The result of this shortage of qualified professionals is that many classrooms are staffed by inadequately prepared or less than competent teachers.

I often ask my second-career graduate students why they did not choose teaching in the first place. The opportunity for a higher salary is the first answer, but the lack of prestige for the profession is another common one. In a survey of other professionals, Friedman (2000) found that half of them did not consider teachers to be in the professional category. Teaching in this country, according to Friedman, has migrated to the position of a semiprofession—perhaps because of the influence of teacher union policies and the lack of self-monitoring or peer review.

WHY THERE IS A CURRENT SHORTAGE: RETENTION

Even after they are trained and hired, teachers have been leaving the profession in unprecedented numbers. The new ones leave for other jobs, the experienced ones retire early. The challenges they face are overwhelming: ever-changing school administrative-position holders and priorities; children accustomed to being left at home alone without adult supervision, soon becoming resistant to any adult direction; competition for engaging student attention from the multidimensional stimulation of modern media; decaying school buildings; increasing occurrences of school violence; the pressure of HSSB tests and publication of the results; criticism from a better-informed group of parents; and, most of all, dealing with all these difficulties in the face of the lack of personal pride one gets from public prestige and respectable compensation.

An overlooked contributing factor to the loss of prestige for teachers is the lack of prestige for teacher-educators. University faculty members in other areas are prone to disparage the role of teacher-educators, and there is often a corresponding inequity in program budgets, faculty promotions, and other forms of recognition. Instead of encouraging promising students to enter the teaching profession, they downgrade that choice. My own daughter, a magna cum laude chemistry major who wanted to be a science teacher like her mother, was thusly dissuaded.

Practitioners—the colleagues and administrators that form the new culture of the beginning teacher—sometimes evince an equally disparaging attitude toward teacher-educators. Novices are quickly confronted with comments that belittle education courses such as, "Forget all the junk you learned in college, because it doesn't work. Here's how to do it."

SOLVING THE PRESTIGE PROBLEM: INTERDEPENDENT STAKEHOLDERS

The solution to the problem of lack of prestige for the teaching profession within the university is a closer interdependent relationship among all faculty working with students, a concomitant recognition of the fact that the future of their culture is dependent on good teaching, and acceptance of the responsibility for preparing all students for the possibility of the teaching task— either as a professional or parent. A possibly unexpected side effect to these efforts is that content area faculty will learn something about teaching their own courses, and teacher-educators will learn something about the content. Later in this chapter, I will describe a personal experience through which this occurred.

A similar solution for the lack of prestige for the university among teaching practitioners is a closer interdependent relationship between the university and P-12 (preschool through 12th grade) schools. Teacher networks are a possibility. A large proportion of my energy as director of the Marie Curie Mathematics and Science Center (MCMSC), St. Thomas Aquinas College, Sparkill, New York, has been expended in developing and nurturing such relationships; some of our programs are described later in this chapter. I will describe the leadership and action roles of teacher networks in Chapter 7.

SOLVING THE PRESTIGE PROBLEM: CHANGING THE AGENDA OF TEACHER UNIONS

Teacher unions in this country have been a powerful force for improving the working conditions for teachers and setting political agendas, but they have not helped build prestige for the profession. Formally recognized teacher unions have not been in existence for very long. At the time I started teaching in the mid-20th century, teacher unions were just beginning to appear. When a move to create one in New York City was initiated, we were recruited in secret. I was optimistic—even walked a picket line. But I soon realized that the union culture, whose purpose was to protect all members, also did little to celebrate those who worked the hardest and achieved the most. In addition, and to the detriment of the profession, it neglected to accept responsibility for those few who gave teaching a bad name. Self-monitoring systems are the hallmark of most professional groups.

The hands-off policy of teachers' unions in the self-monitoring professional role does not necessarily gainsay the feelings of responsibility for the performance of the team on the part of individual teachers. On the very rare occasion when, as principal, I had to make a negative tenure decision, the teachers' union circulated petitions that defended the candidate. My staff signed the petitions but then, in private, told me I had made the right decision. Conflict with teacher union power and prerogatives may have also diminished the hopeful potential of site-based management teams.

I recently had the opportunity to discuss the role of unions with two participants in the Teach for America program, which seeks to recruit outstanding recent college graduates as teachers for urban schools. Candidates commit to teach in public schools in low-income communities for 2 years. Following an expense-paid summer institute, candidates plunge right into a classroom and receive grants or scholarships to cover the cost of future education. Teach for America is a privately funded effort that, over the past 12 years, has placed 7,000 teachers in 16 urban and rural areas. The program provides a critical component of support and comfort, with cohort interaction and mentorship in weekly meetings.

One student I spoke to, originally highly motivated, had decided to leave teaching after 5 years. The other student was still gung-ho. Both cited the excellence of the program but had little to say that was positive about their acceptance into the union-dominated culture of their other colleagues. They were resented, perhaps, because of the "free ride" and special attention but mostly because of their reluctance to stick to union rules, such as those about the number and length of after-school meetings. I will address the issue of leadership by teacher unions again in Chapter 7.

In defense of teacher unions, they have used their power in other productive ways. They have championed the cause for greater public investment in education and even supported the need for higher standards. The late president of the American Federation of Teachers (AFT), Albert Shanker, was a strong and vocal advocate for high standards, although my hunch is that he might not have been as receptive to the extensive, mandated HSSB testing. At the 2001 education summit, current AFT president Sandra Feldman (Wilson, 2001b) reported that support for the standards had, indeed, taken a dive in response to extensive state testing programs. The AFT has, however, consistently maintained their support of state standards and promoted and evaluated them:

> States deserve recognition for their sustained commitment to developing common, challenging standards to serve as the basis for systemic education reform. And states are clearly serious about working to ensure that all their children are exposed to challenging curricula in English, math, science, and social studies. (American Federation of Teachers, 1999, Section II, p. 1)

The AFT has also made recommendations for remediation of existing problems, but these all refer to the investment efforts of others. I would like to propose that teacher unions themselves accept greater responsibility for the existing problems in education today. I do not think taking positive action in this direction is on their present agenda, but they can help!

Although cultural factors are strong contributors to the existing performance gaps, as we shall see ahead, teachers and their schools contribute to almost half the variance in student performance (Suter, 2000, p. 540). Teachers can make a difference, but until unions accept responsibility for teacher quality, we will have to try other means.

SOLVING THE PRESTIGE PROBLEM: RAISING TEACHER SALARIES

Based on an extensive analysis of teacher turnover and shortages, Ingersoll (2001) reveals the self-reported reasons that teachers leave schools either for other careers or different schools. Not surprisingly, the highest percentage of their indicated reasons for leaving was poor salary. One of IBM Chairman Gerstner's suggestions at the 2001 summit conference was to raise teachers' salaries (Gerstner, 2001). Most conference attendees agreed with that approach, especially citing the need to boost salaries in areas of the highest poverty, such as urban and isolated rural school districts. They also favored extra pay for educators in shortage areas such as secondary math and science.

The concept of relating teacher compensation to the performance of students on HSSB tests was less well received. AFT President Feldman (cited in Wilson, 2001b) expressed the union view: "It doesn't make sense. You could have a great teacher working with children who need a lot of help and they shouldn't be held to raising that student to a certain level" (p. 3B). Michigan Governor Engler also expressed concern that this policy would scare teachers away from tough schools (Wilson, 2001a). He may be right, because another strong reason for the departure of teachers, as revealed in the Ingersoll (2001) study, was lack of student motivation. Nonetheless, the lack of pressure for test performance has dissuaded some teachers from joining the exodus from New York City schools to nearby suburbs, where the salaries are much higher but testing pressures greater. However, if those who remain are those who are not competent, the disaster intensifies. The solution is greater rewards for greater challenges and value-added compensation. Can you do better than previously for the same kind of children?

Many conference attendees also were concerned that with the country at war, fewer funds would be available for teacher salary increases. From my perspective, we cannot win modern, technologically focused wars with an undereducated population. Even routing out terrorists requires the intelligent analysis of data.

Raising teachers' salaries should help attract more qualified teachers and is an important first step. Watching my students struggle in their first teaching years and seeing some of them flourish and others fail, however, I am convinced that it will take more than higher salaries to keep them in the profession and growing afterward. The true intrinsic rewards for teachers are those they get from knowing they have reached their students and made a difference for the future. One spark of light of knowing from those whom you have helped out of the darkness lasts longer than a paycheck. We must bring the message of the promise of this reward to capable future teachers, and help new and experienced teachers reach the point of comfort and expertise where those rewards come often.

THE REN MODEL: RECRUITING HEROES

Ideas and attitudes about one's future role in society begin to take shape early in life. Crystallization of career choices may come later, but the ultimate decisions are based on banks of prior knowledge and metacognitive impressions. We need to begin to recruit able and interested students while they are still in high school. We need to provide these young people with teaching and coaching experiences that expose them to the intrinsic rewards of making a difference for others. And, most important, incumbent teachers need to serve as teaching role models for their students. In order to do this well, however, teachers must have respect for what they are doing and consciously convey the message of that respect to their students. The public must reward and celebrate the teaching profession. Why can't we have teacher heroes the way we have sports heroes?

The Teach for America program attempts to create heroes. The Public Broadcasting System produced a widely viewed documentary series, *The First Year,* which depicted the successes and failures of a group of these young people (www.pbs.org/firstyear/, retrieved January 25, 2002). Treatment of education by the media can push students either way. One prime network show that dramatizes the relationships between students and teachers may sometimes lack authenticity, but it certainly can appeal to those who have the need to nurture other human beings. Unfortunately, other media productions may have the opposite effect.

Some successful hero-building actions can be copied from those of the MCMSC program, which is supported by state Eisenhower and National Science Foundation funds. Center-sponsored activities included the Saturday morning Search for Solutions program for 5th to 12th graders mentioned in Chapter 3. Search for Solutions ran for 8 years, was formally validated by

New York state, but then was, unfortunately, curtailed by changing priorities for state funding.

The Search for Solutions program was originally designed as an opportunity to engage greater numbers of female students in science, but its purpose was extended to aim for all underrepresented minorities. Its total enrollment of close to 1,300 students over an 8-year period always included over 50% females, and in the last year, almost half of its 225 students were from minority groups. A salient component of this program was that the groups of students were led by teaching teams composed of practicing scientists working with preservice and in-service teachers or college science professors. Many of the sessions took place at the research institutions or industry workplaces of the scientists. Students frequently expressed their admiration of the interactions among the leadership teams and recognized that it inspired them to engage in the discourse as well. Best of all, they had an increased interest in the possibility of teaching.

The MCMSC has also sponsored over 10 years of professional-development programs for in-service teachers. One of these is Project STEF (Science Teachers Ensure the Future), which engages present science teachers as models for future science teachers. Activities have included

- Strengthening the teachers' own skills with an intensive, research-based and active professional-development experience
- Alerting teachers to the need to inspire their students and others to consider teaching
- Planning direct, teaching-related experiences for their students, such as coaching others
- Promoting opportunities for recognition and sharing among students engaged in science research

In spring 2001, Project STEF sponsored a statewide science congress for students and scheduled the regional meeting of the National Association of Geoscience Teachers (NAGT) for the same dates, creating a joint agenda. Regional student winners, their teachers, and their parents attended the science congress. A group of the best, self-motivated teachers, who were anxious to learn, attended the NAGT meeting. The purpose of the joint schedule was to set the stage for teacher and student interactions in which all were learners. It also served to expose the teachers to the best of student science research and to expose the best students and their parents to the possibility of teaching. Other STEF activities planned for 2002 include A Different Kind of Science Fair, in which students teach others about their research; and a recruitment fair, staffed by incumbent teachers, for possible transitional candidates from other careers.

THE REN MODEL: EDUCATING RECRUITS

Once we have recruited more students, we must then deal with the quality of their undergraduate preparation for teaching. Teacher-educators are frequently blamed for the poor quality of the current pool of candidates even though researchers among them have "substantiated the benefits of what we do" (Sindelar & Rosenberg, 2000, p. 188). Cochran-Smith (2001) alerts us to that fact that "There are also unanswered questions about what it means to educate teachers" (p. 163). Referring to the required accreditation of teacher education institutions, she reminds us that like their public school counterparts, teacher education institutions have had to "shift from input- to output-based programs" (p. 163), taking careful measure of the results of their endeavors.

Teacher-educators should not have to shoulder the whole responsibility. Potential teachers must also be provided with a quality undergraduate education in the content that underlies the pedagogy. College professors need to model the classroom practices that have been proven effective. They need to engage their students more actively in the learning process. We teach the way we are taught. Moving students from college classrooms, where they sit for lectures, to a teaching environment that demands student engagement and inquiry is a difficult transition.

Some recent discussion in reference to this has focused on the relative importance of more content courses versus the need for better pedagogy. Ball (2000) describes the situation as a "persistent divide between subject matter and pedagogy" that "has many faces." "It appears," she continues, "[as] the chasm between the arts and sciences and schools of education or as the divide between universities and schools" (p. 242). Recalling my own experience as a district-level school administrator, I believe the divide also appears in the thinking and habits-of-practice gap between elementary and secondary teachers.

In Ball's opinion and my own, both content and pedagogy are critical and interdependent, and they need to be inextricably combined in programs that prepare teachers, just as the processes and content of the curriculum need to be connected in the classrooms they teach. Uninterested and unresponsive to the new standards, undergraduate liberal arts and science programs rarely actively engage students into inquiry processes related to the subject content, or sufficiently connect what they are doing to actual teaching. The result is that teachers may know the content but "do not know it in ways that help them hear students, select good tasks, or help all children learn" (Ball, 2000, p. 243).

This problem is related to the problem of loss of prestige for the teaching profession. The remedy for both problems may be for universities to create better venues for communication and discourse among the faculties. Effective discourse requires the same language. In an MCMSC summer curriculum development project for college faculty from two separate institutions, whose original goal was to articulate our 5-year program in mathematics and science with that of our feeder community college, I introduced the state's K-12 standards as a basis for coming to consensus. It took a while to interpret the purpose and meaning of the language. Once there was clarity in this, however, the faculties easily came together in subject matter teams to produce a related content and process curriculum that reflected the shared understandings developed in the discourse. Allowing the opportunity for modifications and additions helped facilitate the discourse.

THE REN MODEL: ENGAGEMENT IN ACTION

In another MCMSC progam, which was funded by the National Science Foundation, we teamed education and science faculty with research scientists from the Lamont-Doherty Earth Observatory to plan an early undergraduate science program. The introductory earth systems course was team taught and designed to implement the connections between process and content. The lead research scientist in the group, Kim Kastens, actually audited my graduate curriculum course for a whole semester to learn the language and priorities of educators. Kim's excellent suggestion for making the connections between content and the teaching process was to meet with small groups of students from content courses in follow-up "shadow sessions," in which the students reflected on how learning happened or didn't happen in the previous class.

Piaget (1977) posited that the motivation for new construction of knowledge or accommodations may come from some disequilibrium with prior concepts. Opportunities for students to experience disequilibrium, discrepant events, or dissatisfaction with currently held constructs prepare them to revise, enlarge, or correct these constructs. The curriculum planned by Kim and her team for students in the earth systems course used discrepant data as a focus for the critical-thinking processes required for problem solving and new constructions of knowledge. Research has also examined the differential achievement of students motivated either by task (mastery) goals, which value the outcome of learning for its intrinsic value of knowing, or by performance (ability) goals, which, more egotistically, value the social prestige that higher grades or other evidence brings from comparisons with others. Although both forms of goals may be necessary, in these studies, task mastery goals were associated with more effective performance (Pintrich, Mark, & Boyle, 1993).

Exposing students to real-problem situations in content and pedagogy classes and giving them the opportunity to collect real data or use technologically retrieved data with which to search for answers should increase the impact of task mastery goals and increase learning. This added motivation may also supplement their already existing performance ability goals. Hopefully, this approach will balance the more passive learning experiences of college classes. It may also set the stage for changing the usual single direction of the transfer of knowledge—from professor to student.

THE REN MODEL: ENGAGEMENT IN INTERACTION

Building on Vygotsky's argument that "The true direction of the development of thinking is not from the individual to the socialized, but from the social to the individual" (cited in Lerman, 1996, p. 136), Lerman argues further and firmly for intersubjectivity in the actual acquisition of knowledge. New knowledge is constructed in his view as a shared process. "When an action gains significance for a child (or an adult), becoming bound up with goals, aims, and needs and associated with a purpose, it is a social event" (p. 136)

In the ever-changing informal culture of our modern technological society and its multifaceted media transport system, peers, rather than formally designated teachers, are frequently the social mediators of learning. The importance of culture and informal "doing" endeavors has been established by cross-cultural studies—sometimes comparing small neighboring subcultures—which clearly demonstrate that the informal experiences of varied cultures create disparate abilities (see, e.g., Ginsburg, Posner, & Russell, 1981; Lave, 1977). Perhaps the new knowledge acquired by a large public as a result of the recent events of terrorism is a chilling but prime example. The origins and mechanisms of the spread of anthrax are the topic among a vast and rapidly learning audience of the young and old. Last year, most of these learners would have ignored opportunities to learn anything about this subject.

Although this very effective kind of learning is quite apart and usually different from the formal learning acquired in schools and universities, it is a rationale for the suggested environments of cooperative learning (Johnson & Johnson, 1989). The cooperative-learning environment incorporates the social contexts needed for learning that are implied by Vygotsky (1978) and argued for by Lerman (1996). It enlarges the notion of adult mediation of learning to the recognition of a similar role for peers as mediators—or, perhaps, to a requisite need for a context of interactive discourse and social goals of affiliation as the setting for the acquisition of new knowledge. Preservice and in-service teachers need to interact with each other and learn. Their university professors can also learn with them. Technology has opened vast databases to everyone, and more than one human brain at a time may be needed to interpret them.

An example of the possibilities of shared construction of knowledge is the engagement of preservice students in the collection of their own data or action research. Little strong research reveals the effectiveness of technology in the classroom. For one of the MCMSC activities, I suggested teaming pre-service students and in-service teachers as partners in the collection of real data that would demonstrate how technology was used in classrooms and how it did or did not work. Most important, the opportunity for sharing the construction of knowledge can prepare teachers to use the same kind of moti-vation in inspiring future generations of students to learn. The shared-action research model builds on the concept of intersubjective construction of knowledge. In human interactions, we can learn from each other, but we can also learn concepts that are completely new for each interactor.

Together we must develop schemes for connecting content and pedagogy in college classrooms and guidelines for engaging students in the critical-thinking challenges of real data collection and analysis. Simultaneously, we must engage them in cooperative and participatory experiences with practic-ing teachers from whom and with whom they can learn. Such engagement is a true manifestation of Dewey's (1920/1950) premise that the culture must be renewable. In his own words, noting the importance of connections between means and ends: "Nothing is more intellectually futile (as well as practically impossible) than to suppose harmony and order can be achieved except as new ends and standards" (p. 27). Cohesiveness between under-graduate content courses and education courses will only come with better communication between respective faculties. The end of better preparation of teachers is attached to the means of cohesiveness and communication, just as the means of differentiated analysis of HSSB assessments and responsive reconstruction of curriculum are attached to the end of closing the gaps of student performance.

THE REN MODEL: NURTURING NOVICES

The third element (following recruitment and engagement) of the REN concept is nurturance. In order to attract, engage, and retain future teachers, presenting them with real role models with whom they can work side by side is most critical. Once the teachers are on the job, mentors and interac-tive peer relationships must help them get over the challenging humps of the first years.

As I reflected on my own history in Chapter 1, I recalled how the required daily observation of an experienced teacher and the group discussions we had about the New York State Regents questions were so helpful in getting me through the first high school teaching years. However, in the many subsequent years I spent in teacher faculty rooms, I rarely remember hearing many conversations that dealt with the content or the instructional practices of the classroom. Contrast this with the conversations of the business luncheon, corporate golf game, or scientists sharing data. Unless it is formally scheduled, in-service teachers rarely discuss their methods of instruction. Yes, they do discuss the behavior or performance of individual students but rarely how they themselves structure their instructional time to deal with these students.

In another MCMSC, project we tried to overcome this classroom isolation by engaging in-service teachers in a peer-coaching or peer-interactive process. College faculty worked directly with teams of teachers in a program that directly preceded the curriculum design project we described in Chapter 5. The 120 teacher participants were self-selected peer interactive partners (PIPs) and consisted of an experienced and a novice teacher. The PIPs were charged with following up their initial, shared, formal experience of learning new instructional strategies with interactions during the following school year. They planned together, observed each other, and reflected together in reference to the implementation of the new strategies they had learned together. Their interactive time was actually supported by the allocation of substitute teacher time. There was a further connection to the original experience that was facilitated by the college faculty. The faculty met with the PIPs and their principals on-site to reflect on the progress of their relationships as well as on the implementation of the formal program elements.

When trying new models, it is important to collect the evidence that your model is effective. We collected quantitative and qualitative data to evaluate the effectiveness of this professional-development approach in several ways. In order to measure the immediate effects of the initial formal experience, there were pre- and postexperience questionnaires and reflective papers. These focused on the immediate changes in their understanding of the strategies, on their attitudes toward implementation, and on the nature of the interactions. After a period of time ranging from 6 to 10 months, teachers also completed questionnaires to describe the changes in their attitudes, their implementation of the newly acquired strategies, and the relationships within their ongoing interactions. The college faculty also documented these changes and long-term effects during the yearlong, follow-up site visits.

Data analyses documented increases in the teachers' activities such as joint reflection with colleagues, joint planning and teaching, and mutual observations. It confirmed our hypotheses that the newly learned practices

Table 6.1   Reported Increases in Teachers' Activities

Engagement in observation of colleagues	5.7
Joint planning with colleagues	5.7
Joint teaching	4.4
Joint reflection	6.2
Principal support	6.3
Ideas brought back to grade-level meetings	5.2
Continued meetings with mentoring partner	5.5
Continued use of specific student techniques learned	5.9
Use of a specific lesson learned from a colleague	5.7

Note: On a scale of 1 to 7 with 7 being the maximum increase in activity

would be implemented and that collegial sharing opportunities, such as joint planning and reflection, would be reported as the most common and valuable effects of the entire experience. Validity of the findings was enhanced by considerable agreement between the quantitative and qualitative data sources. The most significant outcome was that not a single novice teacher among the PIPs left the job.

The evidence for systemic change was embedded in two critical concepts:

A. That a collegial system of reflective peer interaction would support continuing professionalism and progenerative (self-renewing) self-improvement
B. That the support of administrators was necessary

Quantitative data collected from teachers in reference to their yearlong engagement in activities that would confirm these concepts are summarized in Table 6.1. Data are reported as the mean of a range from 1 to 7, with a score of 7 representing the highest level of change in the particular teacher activity. Readers may note that joint reflection and principal support showed the greatest increase in activity, and joint teaching was the least frequently increased activity. Later in this chapter, I will describe some of the difficulties and rewards of joint teaching.

The emerging qualitative themes gleaned from follow-up interviews included increases in

- Quality time with colleagues
- Openness with other teachers and opportunity to learn from them
- Sharing of ideas
- Building collegial relationships
- Building professional partnerships

NURTURING EXPERIENCED TEACHERS: THE NEED FOR BETTER PROFESSIONAL DEVELOPMENT

Technology and new information grow at an astounding pace; new HSSB assessments for our nation's schools, increasing gaps between white and minority students, and new knowledge about the nature of how learning takes place require us to *reinvent* teaching and schooling. Understanding and implementing a constructivist approach to teaching, which is not the way that most of us learned in school, is a daunting task. Many researchers, like those I have cited, have identified the professional development of teachers as the key to educational reform. They have also recognized that it will not be an easy task.

Little (1993) explains that although traditional forms of delivery of professional development might work for the skill-training components of reform, especially if transfer of knowledge from experts is followed up with opportunities to practice and is supported by coaching, presently called-for reforms go beyond skills. They require that persons in local situations grapple with what broad principles look like in practice. Grappling then becomes a constructivist, problem-solving experience. It was in the actual construction and trial implementation of their curriculum that we saw our professional-development school partners, the East Ramapo teachers, grapple and learn. And then, their most effective implementation activities were those that correspondingly challenged their students to grapple.

Designing and delivering a curriculum based on rigorous content and performance standards and analysis of required HSSB assessments is a demanding and very different challenge. Just reading about these new ideas may not be enough. Like our students, educators will have to construct new concepts. The commonly used method of delivery of professional development, where knowledge is transferred from experts, might work for the skill-training components if it is backed up by opportunities to practice and by coaching. Nevertheless, it may not be sufficient for presently called-for reforms. Time for interactive reflection with peers and time for guided practice may be necessary (Solomon, 1998). Teachers will need intensive and different professional-development programs to help them with these new challenges. Single-day workshops offered by visiting experts may be inspirational (and I do them often), but they cannot be a substitute for long-term opportunities for teachers to try new approaches, reflect on them with colleagues, and carefully evaluate what they have or have not accomplished.

MOTIVATING TEACHERS TO PARTICIPATE IN PROFESSIONAL DEVELOPMENT

Teachers have to be motivated to participate in professional development that can help them meet the challenges of new standards and HSSB assessments. Stout (1997) identifies some motives that have encouraged them in the past. The first three are

- *Salary enhancement.* Eligibility to compete for extra increments or to climb a career ladder are often tied to participation in staff development.
- *Certificate maintenance.* New York state recently suggested such a policy.
- *Career mobility.* Teachers take courses and degrees and participate in workshops to build resumes. Having done so, they attempt to leave education for other occupations or to pursue other careers within education, administration being the notable example.

Although none of these three motives, in itself, necessarily leads to better performance by teachers, because existing systems do nothing to ensure or encourage it, a fourth motive—their intrinsic wish to gain new skills and knowledge to enhance their own classroom performance—offers the greatest promise. This fourth motive is the critical one, and, therefore, programs that engage teachers more directly in plans for overall school improvement have a greater potential for success. Stout minimizes current existence of this fourth motive, but the vagueness he sees in teachers' commitment is because the extrinsic rewards of the first three motives have clouded the issue, and teachers have not been given the venues in which to develop intrinsic goals.

If intrinsic motivation to improve their own performance is to take over from the other three motives, the nature of traditional engagement of teachers in professional development may need a whole new approach. Smylie (1996, p. 10) identifies some best practices in professional development that have worked. They resemble the things that work with students. They have "a focus on the concrete tasks of day-to-day work" (p. 10) and opportunities to learn that are grounded in inquiry, experimentation, and reflection. They involve interaction with other teachers and are coherent, intensive, and ongoing. We may need to get away from the present marketplace concept of professional development for teachers in which competing graduate programs are disconnected from real needs and from the one-shot conference days and haphazard in-service programs of single districts. Cooperative teaching, professional-development schools, and networking offer this promise.

Teachers' intrinsic goals were clearly at work in the experiences described in the next section.

A COOPERATIVE-TEACHING MODEL

As Lortie (1975) has described, teaching is still very much an isolated task—not too different from the way it was in my one-room schoolhouse. It may be time to break that mold. I believe that shared teaching offers one of the most promising prospects for the creation of new teacher knowledge and skills. Intrinsic motivation provides the energy as teachers share responsibility and discourse with each other in the kernel of their practice, their classrooms. The positive effects of cooperative learning for students have been well documented (e.g., Johnson & Johnson, 1989, and many others). Some have related the success of this instructional approach to the social construction of individual knowledge (e.g., Vygotsky, 1978; Wertsch, 1979), which many have interpreted as essentially a transfer of knowledge from one individual to another.

As we previously described, others such as Lerman (1996) see the social process as a mitigator of the intersubjective construction of new knowledge. Scientists communicate as they share and examine data and together construct knowledge new to everyone. Students in cooperative-learning groups can simultaneously acquire new knowledge.

In an interesting analogy to Vygotsky's "zone of proximal development," which is the place where the adult and the learner's previous knowledge is close enough for new constructions for the learner to occur, Wasser and Bresler (1996) propose the concept of an "interpretive zone" to describe the construction of new interpretations among collaborative researchers. Just as the students and researchers gain new knowledge, pairs or groups of teachers may benefit from the intersubjective construction of knowledge as they straddle or cross an interpretive zone while engaged in cooperative teaching. Cooperative teaching goes an important step beyond team teaching.

In traditional team teaching, pairs or groups of teachers, who are usually diversely specialized, share a common core of students and plan together but, essentially, still work as individuals in reference to time and space. In contrast, a *cooperative-teaching model* goes beyond the sharing of a set of students and planning activities, which is characteristic of team teaching, as it engages teachers in the process of working together with students in the same classroom at the same time. At this juncture of a major effort of school reform and emerging new technologies, we may need to move beyond the isolation and tradition of the one-teacher, one-classroom model. Cooperative teaching promises the potential advantages of better use of time and resources, opportunities for interactive reflections between teachers, greater incidence of teacher-to-student interaction, and the ultimate goal of new construction of knowledge by all in the community of discourse. Doing it effectively, however, will require an understanding of the forces that may mitigate the teacher-with-teacher interactive process.

I had hoped that the implementation of inclusion policies for special education students would foster cooperative teaching. Reports from the teachers with whom I work, however, have not shown this to be the case. Special education teachers and their regular teacher colleagues may be in the classroom together, but, apparently, not as interactive learning partners. Perhaps they need some successful models.

HOW I LEARNED: COOPERATIVE TEACHING

Mathematics teacher-educators have been active in their response to the call for new standards in mathematics education and, in the process, have discovered many cognitive gaps in elementary education students. Some of these gaps lie in the students' own knowledge of the mathematics. In an attempt to fuse the purposes of college mathematics faculty and teacher educators, I became a peer partner in a cooperative-teaching pair. The pair consisted of myself, as a professor of teacher education who specialized in math and science education, and a professor of mathematics (who also was the division head). We undertook shared responsibility for a mathematics course that would satisfy the undergraduate mathematics requirement for education students. In a true model of cooperative teaching, my colleague and I learned intersubjectively and shared an interpretive zone with our students in this new experience.

In the beginning, my partner, Marie, and I had no plan for how we would interact in the classroom. We planned the course outline and met after each class to reflect on the lesson and plan the content of the next. As we interacted with students and each other, conflicts began to develop. Marie spoke in the symbolic language of mathematics. I tried to translate her questions and get the students to verbally translate their answers. I wanted to ask the "why" and "how did you get your answer" questions and search for alternative ways to solve a problem. Marie looked for the right way to do mathematics and the correct answer. We sometimes disagreed openly in front of the students. I was concerned that our previous close relationship was damaged.

Gradually, we began to synchronize; I became more comfortable with her mathematical language, and she began to understand what I was searching for. Some of the students were uncomfortable with the differences of opinion. It was a strange new environment. Others began to appreciate and participate in the discourse. New knowledge (both about mathematics and pedagogy) was created in the "zone of interpretation" as we all parried both in the classroom and in the postclass reflections. In addition to the participant-observer reflections (of both interactive relations and new-knowledge acquisition), our data collection also included formal student evaluations and interviews.

Cooperative-teaching models can range from two individuals sharing time, students, and space to a multiperson team of P-12 staff members planning together, reflecting with each other, and sharing instructional responsibilities for the same group of students. Constraints that participants may encounter include turf and time guarding, competition for student favor and autonomy, and conflicts about expectations for students and their evaluations. My vision for application at the elementary level is a team of three teachers serving a shared class of no more than 50 students. Such an arrangement, in addition to providing opportunities for new knowledge gleaned from shared reflection, would allow for all kinds of flexible grouping of students. Small, individualized groups for remediation or enrichment and larger groups for shared experiences could be easily arranged. The teaming of three teachers would also provide within the schoolday opportunities for professional growth—without the need for substitutes.

PROFESSIONAL-DEVELOPMENT SCHOOLS: OBJECT LINKING AND EMBEDDING (OLE) RELATIONSHIPS

The cooperative-teaching model can also be expanded to cooperation between universities and P-12 schools. Traditionally, universities have used community schools as sites for field experiences in their function as teacher-training institutions, and have made the schools and their people the subjects of their research endeavors. On other, less-frequent occasions, the experts of the university have been brought in to remedy some system problem. Universities have played a substantive, but often unconnected, role in the professional development of in-service teachers. Although this role and the relationship have long been in place, they have, in most cases, been framed in the expert mode with the teacher-educator as the expert and the P-12 teacher as the uninformed novice. Rarely is there a truly reciprocal and ongoing relationship, even though postsecondary teacher-training institutions would be at a great loss without the cooperation of their community schools. Undoubtedly, there were some long-term benefits for the P-12 schools involved in these endeavors. Unfortunately, even these were not always clear, immediate, and measurable.

The closer, more formal relationship of a professional-development school (PDS) may be a remedy. University-based professional-development schools are inching closer to a better or more equitable outcome for P-12 schools involved in well-conceived partnerships. The PDS, in its broadest interactive sense, is a system in which classroom teachers and university faculty work collaboratively to better undersand and improve teaching and learning. Rice (2002) defines PDS collaboration as a "process that utilizes resources, power, authority, interests and people from each organization to create a new organizational entity for the purpose of achieving common goals" (p. 56). This definition sets a worthy goal, but the term *professional-development school* may in itself be limiting because the notion of school represents a defined place. In order to prepare for the technological future, we must envision new but experience-tempered relationships between the university and the schools. We may need to reach beyond limits of place to the concept of progenerative educational webs or networks, where each educator has the potential to learn and respond to the other. The teacher-educator reflects with and learns from the in-service teacher (and principal) and vice versa.

If we think of intersubjective construction of knowledge as what happens in the close interactions among individuals, what happens in a true PDS relationship is an extension of this into interactions among systems. Perhaps we have a metaphor (although an extreme one) for this in computer language. Object linking and embedding (OLE) allows changes made in one system to be automatically transferred to another. In an OLE relationship between teachers and teacher-educators, sharing and reciprocity nurture interdependence and the intersubjective construction of knowledge. The teachers who are at the front line of situational and temporal variations in educational needs, crises, and solutions would assume a greater role in initiating and implementing discussion of needed changes in their own classrooms and in their cooperating schools of education. They would also assume greater responsibility for the professional growth of their peers and novice teachers. An OLE relationship makes sense because, as Sarason (1990) recognizes, "No major educational problem is only a within system problem—that is, arising in and totally comprehensible only in terms of an encapsulated school structure" (p. 35). It makes sense because resources are limited and sharing is parsimonious.

As Sarason and others (e.g., Solomon, 1995) have told us, attempts to implement school change by policy are met with resistance. Measures of policy enactment (such as HSSB tests) ordinarily look for program effects, not for the reasons for the effects, which may or may not be due to the implementation of the policy. The actual mechanisms of compliance are rarely examined, or, as Darling-Hammond (1990) questions, "Was the black box between policy enactment and their measures of policy outcomes opened?" (p. 234). The teacher-educator in a close reciprocal relationship with the teacher effecting change can help open the box and help us understand and deal with resistance. More than that—all can learn together.

Changes will be necessary in such a relationship. New systems of intrinsic and extrinsic rewards for interactive reflection and response may be required for all participants. Time for collaboration, time for change to take effect, and timeliness in respect to conflicting and conjoining priorities will also require consideration. Power will have to be given more frequently and used less often (Solomon, 1995). Leadership can arise from different sources but would require a response and respect. The existing research base for the concepts presented includes foundational findings on the nature and effects of professional-development schools (e.g., Darling-Hammond, 1994; Holmes Group, 1995; Lieberman & Miller, 1986, 1990; Little, 1993).

AN EXAMPLE: THE EAST RAMAPO AND ST. THOMAS AQUINAS COLLEGE PDS

University-based PDS relationships, such as the one previously referred to between the MCMSC of St. Thomas Aquinas College and the East Ramapo schools, are inching closer to a better or more equitable outcome for P-12 schools involved in well-conceived partnerships. The East Ramapo school district is representative of a growing number of suburban schools that are taking on the characteristics of nearby urban districts. Although situated outside a major city, the district is one of the largest nonurban districts in the state, and it has a high-need population that is close to 70% minority.

The very close OLE relationship between the college, East Ramapo, and its neighboring districts has been supported over an 11-year period by a series of New York state education department grants including Eisenhower and Goals 2000 programs. Designation of East Ramapo as a high-need district because of the greater than 50% enrollment of students in free lunch programs has enabled the formation of the more formal PDS relationship with the college. Included in the arrangements are the following connections:

- Consistent and frequent joint planning by district administrative personnel and college faculty
- Nonsupervisory observations of teachers and classrooms by college faculty
- Intensive leadership and engagement of college faculty in district curriculum development
- A college faculty member on the district's Teacher Center Board of Trustees

- Delivery of on-site, district, professional development
- Shared involvement in the solicitation of further funds
- Supervision and staffing of after-school remedial programs by college faculty
- Engagement of teacher education students in intensive district field experiences
- Engagement of district teachers and administrators as adjunct faculty for the college

Wasser and Bresler's "interpretive zone" was rediscovered as we teacher-educators interacted with each other and with East Ramapo practitioners in our curriculum and professional-development planning and work during summer 2001. A growing reality in our state (and nation), and very obvious in the East Ramapo HSSB results, was the "middle school plunge." Promising gains in the 2001 performance of students in fourth grade were compromised by a decrease in scores at the eighth-grade level. The statewide, eighth-grade English passing rate was only 45% at standard or above, but for East Ramapo, it was an average of only 35%. Together, we decided that our first focus would be on professional development at the middle school grade level and in getting better curriculum articulation between the elementary and middle school levels.

ENGAGING IN THE OLE PROCESS

As described in previous chapters, we were engaged in the process of interpreting state standards, designing them down to underlying concepts, and selecting appropriate materials. College faculty and teachers from Grades 4 to 8 met for weeklong summer workshops in three separate teacher cohorts (each separately comprising teachers of math, science, and literacy). We began as whole groups within each subject area and then formed grade-level subgroups. The teachers had been recommended by school personnel for participation in the process based on their recognition as opinion leaders or as highly effective teachers. They were there, however, on a voluntary basis and were monetarily compensated—a grant to the college partially supported this, but the school district added to the stipend.

The district math objectives had been produced the year before and actually coincided exactly with the state-generated "performance indicators." In order to help with consensus building and smooth the transition from existing terminology, we kept the term *objectives*. There had been no previous documentation of science objectives, but a similar design process took the state-generated key concepts down to more specific levels.

Following insightful interpretations of the district objectives and key concepts, and consensus building on the underlying concepts, the teachers organized expectations into more-familiar curriculum units. Although the teacher-educator college faculty members were there to set the stage and help with the interpretations, teachers were given control over the organization of the standards into units and in the selection of materials to pilot. They worked with their peers in and across grade levels to reach consensus and articulation. They will follow up during the year with evaluations of the materials and turnkey training of colleagues—with the help of the teacher educators.

SOME GENERAL CONCLUSIONS ABOUT INCREASING TEACHERS' CAPACITY

One interesting aspect of the PDS potential is that although we teacher-educators were essentially outsiders, we were familiar with one another. Some of the teachers had been our students, and others knew us from their role as supervisors of our student teachers. There are several other significant elements of the engagement interactions described above that are keys to a successful professional-development process:

- Separation of the professional-development process from the supervisory process
- Opportunities for teachers to work interactively with peers
- Utilization of outside but familiar experts to set the stage and provide leadership (they are less threatening)
- Compensation for time spent
- Long-term engagement because through-the-year follow-up is essential
- Consensus-building attitudes fostered by delegation of control (Teachers wrote the specific curriculum units based on the standards, chose pilot materials, and will make the final decisions.)
- Engagement of teachers in research on the effectiveness of the strategies or product
- Engagement of teachers in districtwide dissemination

In addition to pinpointing the factors on this list, I have found, through my long experience with professional development, that the best way to improve the capacity of experienced teachers is to

- Help teachers reflect, using data analysis where possible, on what works best and what does not work well in their current practice

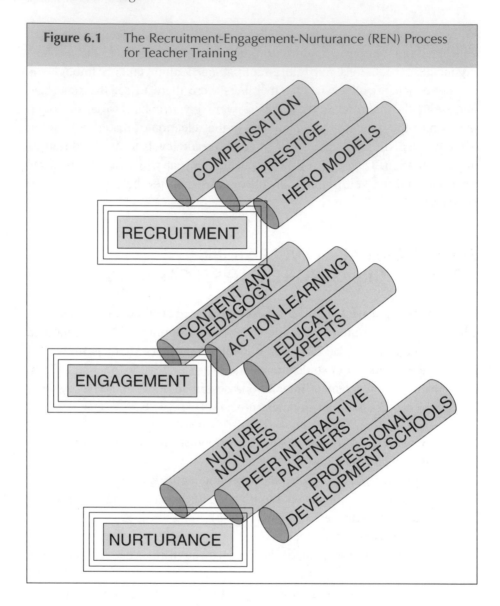

Figure 6.1 The Recruitment-Engagement-Nurturance (REN) Process for Teacher Training

- Expose them to expanded possibilities for making the effective things work better or easier—with the help of models
- Give teachers the courage to discard ineffective practices and try new ones
- Provide encouragement and material support for any change

Figure 6.1 summarizes the REN process. Of course, the success of the process depends on good leadership and other environmental conditions. We will address these final assessment bridge requirements in Chapter 7.

7 Searching for Leadership

ABOUT THIS CHAPTER

A basic premise of the theory of entropy is that things have a natural tendency to move from an ordered state to a disordered state. They run down. That is why housework never ends; we have to return things to order. It is also why schools are either improving or getting worse—they are never static, they are always changing. Improving them requires constant sources of new energy and, often, the energy of effective leadership with power.

If one examines history carefully, we see cycles of change from strong leadership to struggles for more freedom, which sometimes lead to disorder and even anarchy. Then we search again for different leadership. Hitler filled the gap for a Germany struggling with economic depression. The Stalin version of communism helped pull a weakened Russia to success in war and postwar technology. The strong Taliban theocracy of Afghanistan took over when tribal differences created conditions of degenerative disorder. Even a democratic U.S. population welcomed a stronger government role in protecting its security when faced with disaster. Being endlessly searched at airports mattered little, and a president with ambivalent popularity was suddenly respected for sounding strong.

American schools are at a juncture of change from apparent disorder to prescriptions for structure and order. This chapter will try to put the school leadership role into perspective and suggest how effective leaders can take us safely and, hopefully, without the loss of our traditional freedoms, across the assessment bridge.

UNDERSTANDING LEADERSHIP AND POWER

Leadership has been commonly defined in the literature, with minor variations, as "effective influence" (Argyris, 1976, p. 227) or as directing others toward achievement of goals. If leaders influence others, they are, then, effective leaders. Zalesnick (cited in Reitzug, 1994) has added the qualification that leadership "inevitably requires using power to influence the thoughts and actions of others" (p. 284). Power, which may be the broader concept, has been defined as "the basic energy to initiate and sustain action, translating intention into reality; the quality without which leaders cannot lead" (Bennis & Nanus, 1985, p. 17). Power gets things started and keeps them going. Although power itself has also been defined as the ability to control or influence others, we would add *the ability to control one's self and the environment* to that definition. In all cases, power implies the potential for control and for using or releasing energy.

A common conception about power and the ability to influence others is that it must be connected to the ability to dispense tangible rewards and punishments or sanctions, but that may be too limiting unless one includes as reward the intangible satisfaction of complex human needs. Crying infants have power over their parents, and the reward for the parents may be cessation of the crying. But the helpless infant has power over its parents just because of the parents' need to nurture, and school-age children have power over their teachers because of the teachers' imperative to reach students. Teachers, in turn, gain a sense of power when successful at this task. Just having power, however, is a passive or potential energy state. Although it may provide a feeling of satisfaction, it does not get things done until it is used or given away and is responded to.

When power is used to influence others (rather than one's self or the environment) to do something, it connects to leadership. In combination, then, we can define leadership as the active and directed use of power to influence others. Power implies the ability to impose sanctions and rewards. As we have discussed in previous chapters, the recently proposed solutions to the problems of American education have engaged varying degrees and forms of power with and without sanctions and rewards. HSSB tests alone may have some influence but little power. Using them publicly to compare schools and punish those who do not perform are manifestations of a greater power.

The negative reaction of some Americans to this use of power is not unexpected. It comes mostly from those who have not felt the negative results of the lack of strong leadership and, perhaps, its consequence of dysfunctional anarchy in their schools. They are enjoying their freedom to decide how their children are educated and want to keep it that way. It does not come as frequently from undersupported and underperforming urban schools. They may appreciate the benefits of strong leadership. However, in this country, we cannot apply laws differentially. Those communities who revere their independence can make the HSSB tests useful—not as a prescription for what they do day to day but as one of the guides or benchmarks for where they want their students to be at a certain time. This will require leadership.

Simultaneously, those with government power must carefully examine the sanctions they impose to evaluate whether sanctions accomplish the intended goal. Depriving an already underfunded school of needed federal dollars may not solve any problems. The good teachers will go quickly to where they are appreciated. Rewards for good teachers to face the challenges of troubled school environments may be a better solution. Again, we need effective leadership. Can there be effective leadership without power? I think not, but the power need not come from nominal authority or be accompanied by the ability to bestow tangible rewards or punishments.

DIRECT AND INDIRECT MESSAGES

The rats described in the problem in Chapter 1 employed a rather indirect way to get what they wanted: sticking their tails in the bottle and sucking up the oil. Indirect approaches seem to be easier and less threatening. Linguistic researcher Charlotte Linde (cited in Tannen, 1994) has investigated the way we give orders and has come up with some interesting ideas about how we communicate our expectations of others. Giving orders can be either direct or indirect. When the boss says that the place seems dirty today, that boss is implying indirectly that the employee should clean it up. If the boss says, "Get this place cleaned up," that is a direct order. Linde's research also tells us that those in power give both indirect and direct messages to influence the actions of others, but they tend to ignore the indirect messages of others. Those not in power must resort to indirect messages, and they listen and are sensitive to indirect messages. Educators and those who traditionally attempt to influence them are most often indirect.

Politicians, on the other hand, need to be direct in order to appear confident. Once elected as leaders, they also have both nominal power and, through law, the power to impose sanctions. Politicians with a vision, who hold power, may be so blinded by that vision that they give direct orders and neglect to listen to the voices of the indirectly delivered messages of the constituents they represent. Unfortunately, although the current message by politicians to improve schools by imposing mandated testing is a direct message, the substance of the message, like the rat's tail, is a back-ended and incomplete approach. The tail works for oil, but rats need more than oil to survive. Schools will need more than the HSSB tests. They will need leaders who give direct messages but who also listen to the indirect messages of those they lead. They will also need leaders who give the indirect messages of support and the provision of models.

EVOKING CHANGE

If serious improvement of schools is to occur, people must change; but the "paradox of prodding" is that—although real change is self-initiated, people change—this rarely happens without prodding from an external leadership source (Hansen, 1967). The leader who has traditionally been a prodder or evocator of change has been a visionary administrator, university professor, public figure, or government official issuing a mandate. In the recent past, some very recognizable representatives of the latter two forms have assumed evocator roles, including the president of the IBM corporation and the president of the United States. The latter is now preoccupied with a war, but the stage is set, and local politicians are still putting the education crisis at the top of their agendas.

In my hopeful vision, the evocator may also be a teacher-leader responding to internal collegial reflection on present practice (Lieberman & Miller, 1986). Without strength in the role of the evocator who must call forth the change, change will rarely occur. In my three different Pearl River administrative roles—as curriculum coordinator, middle school principal, and director of curriculum—I was the evocator of change. My long history in the school district and the tradition of power in these roles were definite advantages in generating the necessary evocator actions. Consistency without rigidity and a willingness to share power in that role was critical to my success. Unfortunately, there is a tendency in schools for administrators to lead peripatetic lives. They come and go, rarely becoming mature and secure enough in a place to be comfortable with sharing and giving power to others.

Prodding requires the leader-evocator to manage power—either to use it or to give it to others. Tension over the possession of power seems to be an overwhelming characteristic of human civilizations. Although often painful or even devastating, it has not deterred us from progress. Understanding it as a variable, and building that understanding into our planning for change, may make the process and the future more promising. There is always a shift in power attached to the change process, and no one likes to lose power, but sometimes the best way to prod is to give away some power in the form of support. It may be a necessary gift to those who must endure the discomfort of change. At other times, power must be used in the form of pressure.

Visions for improving our schools require support for the people who must change to manifest those visions, but they also may require pressure on people who resist that change. As Huberman and Miles (1984) have told us, a well-balanced combination of pressure and support is usually necessary. Support as a variable of change has traditionally been linked with its complement, pressure. Huberman and Miles (1986, p. 72) actually combine these in what they refer to as "supported enforcement" or, in its sustained form, "assistance." I understand their reason for doing this, but because these variables differ in the way power is managed, it may be preferable for the purpose of definition to separate them. A supporting leader gives power to others. Many of the actions of supporting leaders, however, are the same as the actions of pressuring leaders. Pressure may be viewed as the counter-vailing variable to support only in that a pressuring leader uses power for control instead of giving it. A pressuring leader expends energy and takes some power away from others but may, with complementary supporting actions, indirectly give away some power as well.

In an interesting analysis, Reitzug (1994) also identifies support as an empowering (or power-giving) principal behavior. He identifies the follow-ing forms of support in this behavior:

- Providing facilitation and possibility
- Allowing autonomy with responsibility for supporting practice
- Providing opportunities for conversation with others (which I call peer reflections)
- Providing staff development activities
- Providing tangible and intangible resources, such as time and energy (p. 291)

He adds that a supportive principal would

- Communicate trust
- Honor teachers' opinions
- Ask questions and "wander around" (p. 296)

A pressuring leader will probably not employ some of Reitzug's power-giving actions, such as allowing autonomy, but may still use many of the above actions. I will add to Reitzug's list the important addition of modeling and provide several models in this chapter, but an important point to consider here is that supporting leaders expend their own energy resources and give power to others—it goes into circulation.

Secure people with clear and consistent visions manage power best. Leaders in new positions, dealing with unclear visions not their own, with little direction from above or support from those they are charged to manage, cannot be very secure—especially when their traditional roles are being threatened. While it is true, in contrast, that those in new positions are also the most open to change, sanctions such as complete reorganization of schools may not always be the best remedy. Inconsistent leadership and poor management of power may overcome the intended positive effects.

Sarason (1993) cautions us that we do a poor job of preparing educa-tional leaders. My own training in school administration alerted me to the nature of power and its historical use; but it didn't prepare me for the situation-bound decisions I would need to make, particularly those that required me to choose between the different power components of pressure and support. When I was a novice and insecure, my more impatient inclination— although I always sensed that it was the wrong way to go—was to use my power to pressure others, rather than to give some power away and bide my time with support.

Support, in its many forms, is the safest choice for the evocator; but sometimes pressure is necessary. Each situation is unique, and, quite frequently, we make mistakes. However, there are patterns; knowing them may improve our chances for success. The reader may recognize these patterns from the situations I will describe in this chapter.

LEADING: GIVING POWER AND INDIRECT MESSAGES

Kirst (1995) suggests that leaders and policymakers use a combination of *push* and *pull* factors to help implement new policies. These could be analogies for leadership use of support and pressure. Push factors would include the pressure of HSSB-mandated assessments and graduation requirements that we discussed in previous chapters. Pull factors would include providing the time and structure for professional-development activities such as those we described in Chapter 6. Pull factors require listening to indirect messages and providing support for all the variables that may affect the implementation of a new policy. Sometimes, critical variables are overlooked.

Even the term *curriculum,* in its current interpretation, implies the total school experience. Although the content and performance standards of the curriculum represent a planned vision for the desired results, and the HSSB tests represent a design for measuring these results, neither of these addresses the many other variables that affect what happens in schools: the day-to-day variations in students, teachers, and the classroom environment that together frame the "enacted curriculum" (Ball & Cohen, 1996). In the words of Weinstein, Madison, and Kuklinsky (1995), "Simply willing higher expectations without attention to effective teaching practices will not result in higher achievement" (p. 16). Other aspects of the school environment may require equal or greater attention by leaders. It is the totality of the enacted curriculum that ultimately affects student achievement. The standards by themselves provide a destination without a road map.

Pull factors may include extrinsic rewards such as bonuses or grants for demonstrations of effective practice. However, my experience with teachers tells me that they, just as their students do, respond best to intrinsic rewards.

Knowing that they have reached their students is the reward that makes them try hard to achieve the same satisfaction the next time. Anything that deters the possibility of reaching students has the opposite effect. Pull factors may also include giving teachers some power over their own teaching environment. That does not mean they can ignore the student outcomes needed for the tests; it means that if they have an innovative way to reach those outcomes, they should have the freedom to try it. Glatthorn (2000) agrees and makes some suggestions for principals who are curriculum leaders. Included are the recommendations that they:

- Emphasize mutual accomplishment, not total fidelity
- Present curriculum in a form that provides time and space for teacher enrichment
- Present curriculum in a form that makes it easily accessible, with clearly defined terms and unambiguous objectives
- Not mandate a prescribed sequence or teaching approach (p. 95)

In Chapters 4 and 5, we discussed a form of preparation for tests based on what Popham (2001) called *curriculum teaching*. A leader using curriculum teaching as a pull factor to facilitate preparation for HSSB tests would follow the recommendations in the preceding list. When it is combined with careful interpretation of the underlying concepts embedded in the tests, curriculum teaching gives teachers the power to respond to their own diagnoses of needs.

HOW EDUCATIONAL LEADERS ACT

Contradicting Coleman's (cited in Ornstein, 1975; Suter, 2000) premise that only genetic and cultural factors determine success in school, recent studies have demonstrated the larger influence of teachers and schools. In-depth analysis of variables affecting U.S. performance on the mathematics portion of the Third International Math and Science Study (TIMSS) test show that the class and school are responsible for 45% of the variance in student learning, with socioeconomic factors accounting for most of the rest. The learning environment is more than the written curriculum, more than the assessments, more than the instructional methods and materials, and more than the home environment. The variables combine to create the effect (Suter, 2000, p. 540). Principals are in the unique position to make a difference in the entire in-school environment. And because of recognition and interactions with parents, they may even have a small impact on what happens at home. In repeated research, including that on effective schools, strong principals were demonstrated to be significant positive factors for increasing student achievement (Edmonds, 1983). They are the keys that open the door to school improvement. Can we design a master key?

One of Glatthorn's (2000) premises is that principals do not know how to be curriculum leaders. Does anyone know what makes a good principal? Perhaps principals are not the only ones who do not truly understand the school leadership role. According to Spillane, Halverson, and Diamond (2001), although we have observed what leaders do, the research on how and why educational leaders do the things they do is insufficient. They suggest examining the hows and whys from a distributive perspective. This perspective is based on the concept that each situation is unique and highly dependent on social or shared interactions as well as the material and cultural artifacts (such as buildings, buses, and parent-teacher organizations). The authors believe that because the distributive perspective is grounded in the activities around the interactions and artifacts, rather than in role or position, in order to understand how leadership works, we must examine the macrotasks and microtasks (p. 24).

A PERSONAL ANALYSIS FROM THE DISTRIBUTIVE PERSPECTIVE

Having had a personal experience in three different school leadership roles, I find it useful to reflect on these roles from the Spillane et al. (2001) perspective. In a 20-year sequence as a school administrator, I had the fortunate experience of sandwiching a 7-year middle school principalship between two curriculum roles. In these very different roles, the overall tone of my personal leadership model did not change. I used my power sparingly for pressure and direct messages when necessary, preferring, where possible, to empower others with support. What did change with each role were the situational variables of social interaction—the artifacts, macrotasks, and microtasks. These made the roles and the perceptions of my leadership by others vastly different.

SHARED LEADERSHIP AND POWER

Spillane et al. (2001) note that the leadership role is often shared. Certainly, we easily recognize that kind of sharing among the state and federal leaders. Our Constitution provides for it. At the school district level, boards of education and superintendents jockey for control. As the elective process responds to varying community interests and sometimes single events, boards change and an individual superintendent's tenure in a district is often short-lived. In New York City, following the lead of the former mayor, the present mayor, Michael R. Bloomberg, would like to remove control of schools from the central board of education. Bloomberg and the board's appointed administrator, Chancellor Harold Levy, would also like to eliminate locally elected community boards (Goodnough, 2002).

Less recognized is the fact that in actual practice, such sharing exists at the school level as well. Sharing was an important component of my role as a K-12 curriculum coordinator responsible for science and health, but the nature of the sharing was quite different at the secondary and elementary levels. Secondary principals are accustomed to sharing responsibilities with subject area department chairs and assistant principals. In the middle and high school, I functioned much as a chairperson or assistant principal, responsible for formative evaluations of teachers, supervision of the curriculum, and monitoring of student achievement and placement within the science department. The secondary principals were in charge of summative teacher evaluations, but these were based on the formative ones and we shared responsibility for teacher course assignments.

THE POWER OF MONEY, MATCHES, TRADITION, TIME, AND PLACE

An interesting and less common power split, however, was that the principals were in sole charge of the schedule, but because we were organized on a planned-program budget system, I was in sole charge of developing and managing the program budget. Money brings power. Control of expenditures and the opportunity to argue for program needs directly with the board of education gave me the expanded power of personal interaction as a vehicle for affecting change. Educational innovations are also often initiated by small grants of funds from outside sources. I started a personal pattern of seeking such funds as a beginning school leader and still use them to great advantage in the multiple activities of the Marie Curie Mathematics and Science Center (MCMSC), which I now direct (see Chapter 6).

A great deal of money is not always required to generate and maintain changed practices. Money may be one of a leader's matches, supplying that little bit of heat energy that gets the fire going. The energy is stored in wood but it needs the spark of the match heat to get it released. Educational leaders are like the matches: They have limited power and energy, but if that energy is properly applied, they can get the fire going! Of course, they must stay the course and nurse the fire, ere it quickly dies.

Traditional patterns of leadership are different in elementary schools, where there is no tradition of department chairs. I had little nominal power there except for recommendations, implementation of professional development, and material purchases. Principals and teachers had to be convinced in other ways. Providing the support of money for curriculum materials was one possible way to effect change. Establishing a need and respect for my subject area expertise was another way. The need to prepare for and implement a new, state-mandated, elementary-science testing program helped. Timeliness is another situational variable.

Time, as a variable in the process of change, may be considered from three perspectives: time as a resource to do with what is necessary; time as the component of timetables or the fourth dimension, with which we can plan for, experience, and measure change—or regress to prior states; and time in terms of timeliness, or the probability of success for a new state based on the nature of affecting variables at the particular moment in time (Solomon, 1995).

Timeliness was also a situational factor in my principalship. More formal ideas about shared leadership were just taking hold. Districtwide leadership teams were organized, and my building-leadership team included teachers, parents, and a rotating curriculum coordinator. The team was one of my most effective formal artifacts. It structured the interaction and helped to engage the staff, motivate them to make some necessary changes, and design and implement productive new programs of their own. They, too, soon became the matches.

Place is another situational variable that affects the leader's role in action. While in the peripatetic role as coordinator, my main office was at the high school—although I also shared a place at the central office. Because of this, my own perception of identity or belonging, as well as that of those I led, was more attached to the high school. My significance in other places suffered. The identity of place and sharing patterns were, of course, switched when I became a middle school building principal. Having had the experience of ambivalent identity with place, I appreciated being connected to one place that was mine. And I took that identity seriously. I worried about traffic patterns, buses, broken faucets, peeling paint, and all the artifacts that constitute place. An important point here is that although I had an office at the middle school, I was rarely in it. My staff used to joke that I had worn my own path through the building's halls and outdoor settings. I cheered my students at all the athletic events (I confess to closing my eyes sometimes at the wrestling matches) and got on stage to present accolades for student performers.

I was also in the classrooms. At first, I entered only as part of the formal evaluation system or to deal with some student problem. Soon, however, as trust grew, I was invited to share an interesting lesson or student report. Finally, when the sound of laughter or other clue prompted me to peek through a classroom window, the door was quickly opened for me to share the fun of learning. Leaders are most effective when their place is closest to the place of those they lead.

In the principal's role, I shared leadership responsibilities with an assistant principal and all the subject area coordinators. My only budget was a small one for management. In my final school role as a district-level director of curriculum, I found that the breadth of the responsibility in terms of curriculum decision making and budget allocations, as well as the central office location and closeness to the superintendent, gave me widespread but less direct and, again, multishared power. The beauty of the final role was in the power to analyze the areas of greatest need and spend the needed energy there. I spent much of that power engaged in improving mathematics education.

SOCIAL INTERACTIONS, MACROTASKS, AND MICROTASKS IN CURRICULUM LEADERSHIP ROLES

In each role, the social interactions, artifacts, and tasks of my practice were different. As a science coordinator, most of my direct interactions were with secondary science staff. I concentrated on increasing science course enrollment by changing curriculum and instruction as well as classroom equipment and student placement—and on monitoring instruction and safety issues. The program grew with expanded electives and increased motivation to study science (see Chapter 1). Budget control allowed me to support the focus on inquiry in science classrooms with new laboratories. The simple additional artifact of a full-time lab assistant to help teachers prepare lab materials and control inventory changed the whole direction of day-to-day instruction at the high school. I was right there at the hub of the action, and teaching one class made me part of the group, but the bigger school picture was not yet in my line of vision. Grant money from the state provided a new match. It allowed me to introduce high school career education components in several subject areas, and the scope of my influence and responsibilities grew (Solomon, 1980).

At the elementary level, my first task was to establish a positive interactive relationship with the elementary principals. They were suspicious of my central-office connections and high school origins. An earlier 4-year experience as an elementary teacher only helped a little. The new state tests were timely tools that formed the basis for interdependent discourse, and I found a lucky artifact: the National Science Foundation–supported Science Curriculum Improvement Study (SCIS) program. Together, the principals and I identified two teachers who were strong opinion leaders, and I brought them with me to Michigan for training. They helped me sell the inquiry-based

SCIS elementary science program to principals and their teacher colleagues. Together, the original teachers and I trained the other elementary staff members to use the very different approach to teaching science. The program as an artifact helped as it won the teachers and the students over with crickets, chameleons, and butterflies. My microtasks included keeping the accompanying kits supplied and even raising crickets in a closed pail of dog food stored in the custodian's closet.

The responsibilities for the health program took me into a different set of social interactions. The home and community were too strong an influence not to matter. I met with parent groups to share successful strategies for dealing with sex education for preteens and structure for their rebellious teens. I spoke to the local Rotarians and, with their encouragement, formed a community group to counteract the growing drug and alcohol problem. I gathered and used evidence from our own statistics on abuse to justify the energies expended. With the group's help and a small grant of county funds, we opened an after-school center for the teens so they could have a supervised, but unstructured, place to hang out. Video games, music, and couches, as well as a place to get some homework done, were substituted for drinking beer on the high school fields.

In my later role as director of curriculum, timeliness forced me to confront a new issue: AIDS education. The interactions had to include local clergy, parents, and teachers. Together, we developed a plan of action. Even in our predominantly Catholic community, the need for extension of what kids learned about sex was recognized and accepted. What a surprise when an opposition group I had not realized existed suddenly emerged at our board of education's finalization meeting. A small cluster of Christian fundamentalists raised some objections. I had neglected to include them!

The artifact of districtwide assessment data and the task of disaggregated analysis (Chapter 4) helped me recognize the deficiencies in mathematics education that I began to describe in Chapters 3 and 4. Careful analysis of the existing program showed that the problems began at the elementary school with too much emphasis on procedural drill and practice and too little on concept development. At the high school, it was low expectations on the part of teachers, students, and even their parents.

I initiated my macrotask of program improvement by trying to get the elementary and secondary groups together in an attempt to engage them in the change process. All hell broke loose at our first meeting of interested volunteers. They blamed each other for the deficiencies. The high school teachers blamed the elementary ones for not preparing students, and the elementary teachers blamed the high school teachers for not caring about those who were not succeeding. Ultimately, they all recognized their own ends of the problem and, with my support, pursued corrections. Fortunately, the high school building-leadership team had just embarked on a schoolwide mission to increase expectations—and two math teachers were on the team.

At the elementary level, the next macrotask was professional development to introduce a constructivist perspective. A preparatory round of spring visits by elementary teachers to other schools with constructivist programs was followed by a summer workshop for this leadership group. As a culmination of the workshop, I gave the teachers the right to choose which of the observed programs they wanted to pilot—even if it was more than one adoption. They chose a common and interesting alternative of their own program using a variety of mathematical manipulatives (concrete, representative materials) and a concept-oriented new text. They were given a budget to order the mathematical manipulatives. We also planned for follow-up, formal, inservice components, and reflective sessions in the fall.

The manipulatives were remarkable artifacts. They helped the teachers understand the constructivist perspective and learn new concepts themselves. Nonpiloting teachers were jealous and the following year jumped anxiously on board. My microtasks included buying, making, and modeling their use. At first, I did most of the modeling, but soon, the leadership team modeled for their peers in regularly scheduled rounds.

The final step was a jointly written curriculum, with specific concepts stated. It was very much like the form of curriculum suggested in Chapter 5 and, in fact, ultimately, became the framework design for my book *The Math We Need to "Know" and "Do"* (Solomon, 2000). Having a written curriculum as the framework for instruction is a critical artifact. It frees instruction from the boundaries of a particular textbook. Teachers were encouraged to use multiple supportive materials, including many of their own design but based on the goal of reaching understanding of the explicitly stated concepts in the written curriculum. Some of the difficulties in neighboring districts that implemented mathematics reform by adopting a textbook program as an unrelenting entity may have been due to the fact that it deprived teachers of their power to use what worked for them. Any unfavorable publicity for an imported program that is used in many places can also be destructive. Curriculum that is owned by those who use it is the safest and most effective. That does not mean that owned curriculum cannot use imported materials. They become the resources of the curriculum and sit beside those that teachers invent.

Data can be an important leadership artifact and examining it as a peer group a critical macrotask. Following the first year of implementation of the math program, we looked at student achievement data that compared the experimental pilot group and its control group of classes taught by nonpiloting teachers. We also looked at teachers' answers to surveys that evaluated the compared programs. The data helped convince everyone to expand the new program to every classroom.

At the high school, teachers also examined the data, which included participation rates and surveys of teachers, parents, and students. It showed lack of participation in upper-level courses and poor expectations, complicated by early and excessive tracking. We had five different courses for ninth graders, and only 40% of the population went on to a third year of math. The success rate of those who took the third year was also dismal—only 60% passed the state Regents examination. Our remedy was to eliminate the ninth-grade, non-Regents track for most students and, instead, provide extra support for needy students in the way of small classes and an extra math period of small-group work led by a teacher and an especially capable teaching assistant. Two experienced teachers volunteered to teach the classes. Within 3 years, enrollment in third-year Regents classes doubled, as did the success rate on the tests. The long-term positive results are clear, as previously reported in Chapter 4. The implementation process is explored in greater detail in one of my previous books (Solomon, 1995).

At each level of the curriculum role, the most critical macrotask was my effort to engage teachers and principals in the decision-making process. It ensured ownership, which is a vital component of the REN model we discussed in Chapter 6. It also was a prevailing theme for my role as a building principal.

SOCIAL INTERACTIONS, MACROTASKS, AND MICROTASKS IN THE PRINCIPAL LEADERSHIP ROLE

As a building principal, I found that the bigger picture took over. The larger artifacts and tasks that were implements of power to change instructional practice included the schedule, which is a powerful mitigator of change, the reporting system, and organization of teaching teams. Other large and influential macrotasks included the physical conditions of the school environment, expectations for student behavior, parent relations, and public image. Small artifacts, however, can sometimes be significant. When I took over, the school had a reputation as "the zoo." Students wandered the halls between classes, the lunchroom and play period were a disaster, graffiti covered the walls, and student motivation to learn and teacher morale were low. Hazardous traffic and busing patterns compromised safety, and the nurse's office was a constant hub for the lunchtime accidents.

My own previous experience told me that a first step would have to be to establish a more orderly environment for learning—one that was safe and one where student and faculty had respect for the place and then the content of learning. I wandered the halls and delivered students to embarrassed teachers, who had not reported their absence. Assigning students to lunch tables, pulling them out of class to clean them up if they left them dirty, and shortening the lunch period to 30 minutes made a big difference. I used a schedule adjustment to substitute extra physical education time for the free playtime lost. Although my messages to students were direct, most of my messages to teachers were indirect: "Watch me as I model what needs to be done."

A building-leadership-team subgroup that consisted of teachers, some parents, and me developed more formal rules for behavior. They were approved by the entire faculty and were a consensus of what was needed and realistic. They were published and interactively shared with students and parents. At the beginning, there was some hesitation, but everyone soon saw the benefits. My students gave me a military salute as I drove past the bus stops in the morning. An angry parent called me one day to protest that I had made the entire sixth-grade class clean up some graffiti, which had mysteriously appeared in their play area during lunchtime. He argued that his child had not done it and should not have been required to clean it up. I asked him to come to see me and showed him pictures of the before and after conditions of the building, took him around to see classes in action, and asked which school (the before or after) he would prefer for his son to attend. He did not hesitate with his answer and left as a supporter for my cause.

Next came the concentration on curriculum and instruction. The curriculum coordinators helped as we shared plans for professional-development components, but a schedule change that gave team teachers common planning time allowed so much of it to happen. Teachers were much less stressed as student behavior got better, and motivation to learn, along with motivation to provide a variety of learning experiences, increased. Student performance on standardized tests improved, as did the school's reputation. There was one continued deficiency that annoyed me constantly—the mathematics program. I sometimes even pulled a struggling student into my office to try to help. "Too much time spent on worksheets and not enough on understanding what you are doing" was my analysis. But I did not have the time or the power to make enough difference—it would have to wait until my next role as a districtwide curriculum director.

We took the incoming sixth graders on a 3-day camping trip to establish relationships and provide a field-based nature experience. School plays, dances, musical performances, academic competitions, and awards assemblies established changed value systems. Learning could be fun, but it was also worth working for. The children trusted the adults, and they trusted each other. A student-run, peer-mediation committee was formed, trained, and soon successfully settled student disputes and some minor school rule infractions.

I did not abdicate. I was there at every function, first to arrive in the morning and last to leave. Even the tiniest little "micro tasks" (Spillane et al., 2001) made a difference. I noticed that the custodian had lowered the level of the drinking fountains one very warm June and asked him why. He said that because the children were using them so frequently, there was often water on the floor. I gave a direct message: "Raise them," I said. "I'd rather have the water on the floor than dehydrated kids spreading germs as they mouth a barely trickling faucet."

Most of our students were bused to school, but teacher union negotiations had removed bus duty from the teachers' responsibility. I was out there every day with just a few teacher assistants and my assistant principal. One afternoon, as close to 500 students were lined up to board the buses, a mini-tornado hit the area. We struggled to get the children inside, but the suction prevented us from opening the doors. When we finally got them open, we threw the screaming children inside. Fortunately, no one was seriously hurt, but not one teacher came to help. At a faculty meeting the next day, I told the story of our travail. It was only an indirect message of interactive leadership delivered without demands. It was, however, heard. From that time forward, teachers appeared at the bus lines whenever the weather was bad.

The focal point for what made us work and learn well together was that everybody cared, and our students trusted us to nurture and protect them. I have saved a particular note from a student that for me sums up the results of that element of my leadership model (Figure 7.1). It was an anonymous type-written request for me to enforce a senior-seventh-grade privilege—sitting at the back of the bus.

THE SHORTAGE OF ADMINISTRATORS

Reflecting on my own experience does not make me regret one moment of the time I spent as a school administrator. Nevertheless, given some of the new challenges faced by our formal leaders, it is not difficult to understand the current shortage of candidates for this critical role. A large part of the problem is that those who already serve retire early or leave for easier places. In New York City, two out of three principals have fewer than 5 years of experience on the job, and 36% fewer than 2 years (Holloway, 2001). Many of the retirees were born just before and during the early years of the postwar baby boom. They became the teachers of the 1960s and 1970s (some to avoid service in the Vietnam War) and then, the principals of the past two decades. Gilman and Lanman-Givens (2001) have examined the reasons for this shortage. To begin with, the ranks of teachers are the usual sources for educational leaders. Teachers are, however, becoming less willing to apply, dissuaded by diminishing pay differentials between themselves and administrators; the

Figure 7.1	An Anonymous Request From a Student Who Trusts a Principal

Dear Dr. Solemn,

I know you have talked to thr 5th and 6th graders before but they are in the back again and when weget on the bus we tell them not to sit there but they still do. When we get to the biggest bus stop which has most of the 6th and 7th graders all the 6th graders come back and dont leave any room for the 7th graders,like my best friend Brenda, and my not so best Juile and now there stuck in the front or middle of the bus with the 5th graders and we cant talk to them and after school they sit inthe second to back (in the moring they sit in the second to back to we tell them not to but they wont listen) We ask them to move in or let you sit with them but they wont let them, would you please mabey when were all on the bus come on see and see where they sit PLEASE because I'd really like to talk to my best freind and not so best friend Brenda and Juile, You can even ask Brenda and Juilehow they feel about sitting there because they will probaly tell it stinks because they cant sit in the back.I dont want to say my name or everybody will hate me.

Sincerelyyours,

A student from busA.M. bus7 p.m. bus 6

burgeoning cost of obtaining credentials; the many pressures of accountability, politicians, parents, the media, and other special interest groups; and the responsibility for maintaining standards. All these new pressures add further to the many artifacts and tasks I have described from my own experiences.

Most of Gilman and Lanman-Givens's (2001) recommendations for overcoming the shortage of administrators resemble the recommendations for recruiting teachers. In addition to higher pay, they suggest mentors for novices, more relevant preparation programs from universities, active recruitment, and restructuring of the principal's role toward more time for instructional leadership and less time on managerial duties. Assistance from others, such as assistant principals, and more authority to make their own decisions are also recommended. In addition, I recommend a stronger role for teachers in school leadership. It worked for me. Administrators must, however, give teachers the power and authority they need, and teachers, in turn, must accept the responsibility for productive use of that power.

LEADERSHIP BY TEACHERS

Throughout this book and earlier in this chapter, I have shared my vision that teachers have the opportunity to make decisions and take responsibility for leadership roles. Unfortunately, until they also assume responsibility for monitoring the performance of others, the effects of teacher leadership will be moderated by those who have the power and accept the responsibility. As previously discussed, teacher unions have played a role in the support of higher standards and expectations and also in acting as a voice to express the interests and often-unheard indirect messages of the teachers they represent. This is a vital role, but it misses the professional self-monitoring components of a bar association or medical practice board. Unions have also fought the introduction of merit pay. If there are no sanctions and no rewards for individual teacher performance, there is little power to affect individual performance.

An interesting new venue for teacher leadership that is most effective in the East Ramapo schools and in other places is the teacher center. This entity is structured as separate from the teacher union and funded by the state. I actually serve on the East Ramapo Teachers Center Board of Trustees, as do teachers, administrators, and a board of education member. Freed from the us-against-them atmosphere of the union and administrative supervisory demands, the teacher center has been most effective in providing the support and reward functions missing from the union organization. Its activities include

- A mentor program for novice teachers
- Homework center and hotline
- A professional resource library and videotapes
- Laptop loans
- Meeting facilities
- Minigrants
- Assistance in writing the grants

The East Ramapo Teachers Center has its own Web page that can be accessed at www2.lhric.org/ertc/ (retrieved February 2, 2002).

LEADERSHIP BY TEACHER NETWORKS

An expansion of the teacher center concept can also be found in teacher networks, which sometimes add the component of university-based teacher-educators. Teacher networks are also a broader extension of the professional-development school relationship we discussed in Chapter 6. Networks are a prime example of productive shared leadership. They have appeared in several different forms. There are privately funded and university-affiliated networks such as the New Standards Project and the Center for Research on Evaluation, Standards, and Student Testing (CRESST). Other successful networks include the Philadelphia Alliance for Teaching Humanities in the Schools (PATHS), the Urban Mathematics Collaboratives, and the National Writing Project.

After a study of networks that are part of the National Center for Restructuring Education, Schools, and Teaching (NCREST), Lieberman (1996) reports that the opportunity for sharing among teacher-participants

> Has the effect of dignifying and giving shape to the substance of educators' experiences. . . . Networks are particularly good at helping school-based educators discuss and work on current problems . . . teachers and administrators find it easier to question, ask for help, or tell it like it is. (p. 52)

She describes leadership in networks as making phone calls, raising money, arranging meetings, brokering resources and people, and negotiating time commitments for university- and school-based educators. Lieberman is right on the mark! That is exactly what I have to do to bring about the MCMSC activities. These actions can be further framed in terms of interactions, artifacts, and tasks.

Lieberman (2000) notes that "although many educational institutions are not sensitive to developing norms of participation and organizational support as necessary conditions of learning," the networks pay attention to this need, and the actions of sharing and participation "released great power and energy" (p. 223). The strength of these groups is based on several aspects that include capacity for teacher support over and above the single district or university, norms of informed experimentation, a system of mutual aid (mentoring) that compensates for uneven preparation of teachers, connections to the classroom, and engagement of teachers in professional discussion and debate (Little, 1993).

The MCMSC network is the venue for the many programs that have already been discussed in this book. It is much smaller than the networks mentioned above, but it is now entering its 11th year. The network started as an outreach from a college graduate education program to the surrounding schools. Its original focus was in math, science, and technology education, but with increased funding, we have now extended to programs in literacy and equity. The center has provided in-service support for teachers and an enrichment program for students in Grades 5 to 12. The network has several important distinguishing characteristics:

- An advisory board comprises school district administrators, teachers, parents, students, college faculty, and industry representatives.
- Through peer coaching in the in-service programs, teachers learn how to engender trust and interact with each other for the purpose of instructional improvement.
- In most cases, teachers must sign up with colleagues. The districts recruit participants in what we call Peer Interactive Partners (PIPs).

PIPs are made up either of two experienced teachers or an experienced teacher and a novice.

- Connections exist between the program elements. It becomes a learning laboratory. Follow-up, on-site, reflective meetings are held in the districts with college faculty members, participants, and building administrators. College course practicums are held at school sites where preservice teachers work with district students.
- Experienced teachers who participate are also eligible to become paid supervisors for the student teachers.
- Cooperative teaching in the student program most often features a PIP of scientist and teacher but sometimes a pair of teachers.
- Cooperating members of local industry have provided us with venues, materials, and personnel for the student and teacher programs.
- College faculty members are learning participants in in-service programs alongside P-12 teachers.

The MCMSC network includes all the school districts within an entire county and several in neighboring counties, local teachers centers, and St. Thomas Aquinas College. Recently, it has reached out to work with other higher education institutions in joint programs, including a local community college and the earth sciences graduate school of Columbia University's Lamont-Doherty Earth Observatory, which is a nearby neighbor. Support comes from some private sources, the districts, the college, the state (using federal sources), and the National Science Foundation. MCMSC is, therefore, accountable to each policy-making entity to some degree, but essentially, agendas are designed by the leadership team, shared, and approved by consortium members. The leadership team plans and monitors all activities. Instructional staff for the programs includes teachers, principals, college faculty members, outside consultants, and scientists from a local research facility.

MCMSC provides monetary incentives in the form of stipends, but these rarely match regular pay. Another incentive is the possibility of getting graduate credit at a reduced cost. About a third of the teachers opt for this. The school districts have also agreed to offer in-service credit, and another third of the teacher-participants usually ask for this. In addition to long-term programs, there are also single-day workshops planned for dissemination and introductory purposes.

MCMSC NETWORK: SAMPLE ACTIVITIES

One of the MCMSC professional-development programs was organized around a long-term, reciprocal relationship. It had structured interactions among teaching peers, their principals, and teacher-educators. The historical pattern of teachers coming into the college for a formal instructional program and then completely disjoining from it was altered in this program—but the formal component was not completely abandoned. The concept of the teacher-educator as the expert and the practitioner as the learner was also transformed in this innovative program. The teacher-educators were engaged in the beginning, formal experience as students alongside the teacher-practitioners. Expert practitioners acted as the instructors or learning leaders. They had previously participated in an effective-teaching-strategies model at the center, and this was the core of the formal instructional component.

College faculty members organized the beginning, formal-training component and recruited and supervised the instructional staff (made up of school administrators and expert teachers). The training consisted of 35 hours of small- and large-group activities that illustrated teaching concepts such as clarity, attention, momentum, time and space, classroom climate, and expectations. There was also an important session on how to be an interactive peer coach. The 120 teacher-participants were self-selected PIPs partners, and each pair consisted of an experienced and a novice teacher. Four college faculty members were also participants.

The formal component was only the beginning. The PIPs were charged with following up their initial sharing experience by planning together, observing each other, and reflecting together in reference to the implementation of the new strategies they had learned together. The interactive time was actually supported by the allocation of substitute teacher time. There was a further connection to the original experience that was facilitated by the college faculty. The faculty met with the PIPs and their principals on-site to reflect on the progress of their relationships as well as on the implementation of the formal program elements.

In Chapter 5, I described another follow-up activity in which teachers from nine different school districts were recruited for another interdistrict, curriculum-writing endeavor that addressed new state standards in math, science, and technology. Again, we initiated the macrotask by bringing the participants who represented all grade levels and the college faculty together for 4 summer days to prepare them to write the curriculum that they would then use and share with others. The 4-day preparatory program took them through a rotating schedule of technology and curriculum-writing components. The instructional staff consisted of a combination of technologically expert teachers, curriculum-oriented school administrators, and college faculty.

Included in the leadership tasks of both these endeavors was a spectrum of short- and long-term evaluations. There were short-term assessments of new knowledge, long-tem assessments of implementation (via site-based interviews), and evaluations of the product (curriculum).

WHAT WE LEARNED
ABOUT LEADERSHIP NEEDS

Surprisingly, there was little relationship between the self-assessments done immediately after the formal instruction and those done after 7 or 8 months of implementation and curriculum writing. And there was no relationship between the level of the quality of the curriculum documents produced and the first assessment. There was a significant correlation between the final self-assessment and the quality of curriculum. These results told us several things. To begin with, we learned that:

- Short-term professional-development endeavors that have no application followups are short-lived. Leaders have to plan for long-term engagement.
- Confronting the creative task of writing curriculum and implementing it may have changed the self-perceptions of what was learned and helped the final construction of new knowledge. You learn best by doing. Action learning works best. It must be planned for.

Qualitative data collected in follow-up interviews may also indicate why some perceptions changed to the positive. Some activities teachers thought would work did not, but many exceeded their expectations and brought them satisfaction. Publication of their work on the Internet also helped their feelings of efficacy. Intrinsic rewards are long lasting.

Corcoran and Goertz (1995) may have an explanation for over-time changes toward the negative. They identify inappropriate sequencing of program implementation as a common problem. Several of the districts had not yet acquired the software or updated the technology that participants had experienced in the workshops and had planned for in their curriculum. Even if it was in place, some could not get technology access when they needed it. The level of support our participants received from home schools varied and affected their final assessments. Some of the teacher-participants reported that the central office and building administrators had different opinions on whether or not the new standards were worthwhile. Leaders who share power and responsibility must plan in tandem and pay attention to sequencing. Many teachers are now overwhelmed by the demands of HSSB tests. Poor planning and sequencing by educational leaders is at fault. Evocators of change did not pay attention to the prevailing artifacts or engage in the appropriate interactions and tasks.

ADDRESSING SOCIOCULTURAL NEEDS: OTHER SOURCES AND FOCUSES OF LEADERSHIP

Although I do not wish to underestimate the importance of the variables of schools, teachers, and their leaders, the sociocultural influences of the home, peers, and society are responsible for over half of the variance in student performance (Suter, 2000, p. 540). Principals can help their students by establishing systems for strong and comfortable interactions with parents and other cultural entities. Principals can help by establishing systems for strong and comfortable interactions with parents and other cultural entities. A county-managed adult mediation council explained the role of our peer mediators to parents (and helped train the kids). Another community group addressed the issues of setting guidelines for at-home behavior. The police department introduced the Drug and Alcohol Resistance Education (DARE) program that helped us with drug education. Multiple forms of engagement and willingness to share work best.

Parents participated in building-leadership teams; they helped plan, and came with us for our 3-day, outdoor camping experience; and they cheered the academic competitions (science Olympiad, spelling bee, etc.). The artifacts of reporting to parents on the progress of their children are critical. When our building-leadership team decided that we needed to change our report cards to add items that represented some of the new interpersonal values and constructivist emphases, parent committees were involved in the reforming process. One bit of advice that I often offer teachers is to set up the first personal parent communication early in the school year with a positive note, before the need for a negative one develops. It opens the lines of communication, and sometimes a bit of information interchanged can prevent the need for a negative one.

In some cases, directed parent education is important. In the first year of our districtwide implementation of the new math program, I offered a 10-session opportunity for parents to learn about the change and perhaps to relearn their math concepts. We had one section in the afternoons and one at night so that working fathers and mothers could come. For the afternoons, we arranged for baby-sitting. At the first session, I gave the parents a 10-question test of math problems but did not allow them to write anything. Naturally, they were frustrated with the challenge of mental arithmetic. Brief explanations of how every problem could be calculated mentally were a revelation to them. I simply said, "If your children are exposed to our new methods, these kinds of skills will be part of what they do in school and, more important, in everyday life." Because of this extension to parent education, we had little of the public response difficulties in our implementation of mathematics reform that our neighboring districts experienced.

The omission of vision sharing and parent education was a serious mistake on the part of leaders of our current push for HSSB tests. In an interesting study, Goldenberg, Gallimore, Reese, and Garnier (2001) discovered that although invariably high, Hispanic parents' aspirations for their children were unaffected by the messages they got from the schools, while their expectations for their achievement were responsive to those messages: No matter what reports came home, Hispanic parents still wanted their children to achieve and aspire to high goals. Their confidence that the goals would be reached, however, was diminished by negative reports from school.

COMMUNITY-BASED LEADERSHIP: PROJECT EEXCEL

Project Eexcel is another MCMSC activity that connects schools, community, and teacher education. Steve Fetner, a builder who had constructed a low-income housing project in the East Ramapo Haitian community, originated Eexcel. He sought my help in getting the after-school center he had envisioned as part of his project. Together, we planned how the center would work, hired a manager, and equipped a wonderful space within the project with computers, books, and comfortable learning spaces. Grant funds helped us get started. The children come there after school and get help with their homework and other needed remediation. They also can hang out for a while or play chess. Preservice teachers from the college and other volunteers work at the center. It provides a safe and supervised place for the children of the mostly immigrant and working African American parents. Working at the center gives the preservice teachers opportunities to interact with minority kids—and it gives the children positive role models. Parents participate on an Eexcel advisory board and support the center's value-based emphasis on the importance and joys of learning.

COMMUNITY-BASED LEADERSHIP: WINDHOVER FARM

I began this book with a personal reflection on my early life on a farm. Serendipity takes me back to that very place. In a moment of nostalgia, I took my own grandchildren to the farm that I had not visited in over 50 years. There I found Father Matthew Foley, a priest from Williamsburg, Brooklyn, who is now its owner. Father Foley has an after-school program much like Project Eexcel that he runs out of his home parish. But on weekends and in the summer, he brings his troubled youngsters from the Brooklyn ghetto to the farm. When they are there, they develop a sense of family and interdependence missing from ghetto life. The values and motivation are also different. The children also learn from the same real-life experiences I addressed in Chapter 1.

Father Foley is full of wisdom, but one remark sticks in my mind. "Before I can help these children learn, they must be ready to listen." The listening pattern he has to overcome is the one in which the role model messages of the streets of the ghetto supersede the role model messages of missing parents and sometimes unprepared teachers. The crew of former visitors who are now productive adults is evidence of Father Foley's success in this endeavor.

The children also learn traditional things in a different way. They sit around an open fire and tell stories or read books together; they study and care for the living things on the farm and sometimes bring them home to study more. Everyone has a job and some responsibility for others. I have brought my own preservice students to Windhover Farm to help, teach, and learn. We do our science lessons in the field, using the pond, forest, and fields of my own youth as a habitat. The frogs are the many-generation descendants of those I caught, and there is still a blacksnake den in the same spot behind the barn.

USING MODELS TO BUILD THE ASSESSMENT BRIDGE

The children and the time are different from that of my childhood on the farm and the problems of our present overwhelmingly greater. Nevertheless, there may be other leaders, such as Steve Fetner and Father Foley, in unexpected places and models in expected places from whom we can learn. Private organizations are also becoming engaged. Organizations such as the National Association for the Advancement of Colored People (NAACP) have taken up the cause of higher standards. The WK Kellogg Foundation (www.wkkf.org/, retrieved January 28, 2002) invested $28 million dollars in an effort to work with communities to boost the enrollment of Hispanics in college.

In addition to addressing curriculum and engaging teachers in professional-development programs, some schools are themselves engaging in actions to address sociocultural differences. Kahlenberg (2000) tells of a Wisconsin superintendent who turned a failing school around by changing its boundary and that of a higher socioeconomic school to include a better mix of children from high- and low-poverty areas. Minnesota may be able to provide a model for the curriculum reconstruction part of the challenge. The level of the state's student performance on the eighth-grade science portion of the Third International Math and Science Study (TIMSS) test was surpassed only by

Singapore. They attribute their success to a long-term consensus on their science curriculum and on its concentration on in-depth learning rather than on broad coverage of many topics.

In a discussion of how principals can be leaders who provide inclusive education for diverse students, Riehl (2000) suggests that they are the "key agents in framing" and communicating new meanings, and that a key strategy for accomplishing this is the "promotion of democratic discourse within the school community" (p. 61). Our educational leaders can help us build our bridge!

Faced with insurmountable obstacles, humans have built successful bridges and tunnels by using their superior ability to think, reason, learn from prior experience, plan, experiment—and then apply their knowledge to the final construction project. Never was this accomplished without individual energy expenditures, sweat, and the pain of interim failures. With time, patience, a reflective examination of the successful models of the past and the present, and a few sparks to light the fire that stokes the engine that produces the asphalt for the final roadway surface, we can build our assessment bridge. We can close the achievement gap and create a passage to an educated culture, and we can make that passage stronger, less stressful, and more secure for every child who crosses over.

Epilogue

In the brief period since I started this book, the primary focus of the citizens and government of the United States has unexpectedly and profoundly changed. The headlines on tests and standards left the front pages for a while. The problems, however, are still there and assuredly will again surface to the

Figure E.1   The Group, III

SOURCE: Copyright © 2001 by Hilda Epner. Reprinted by permission.

limelight. The remarkable response of this country and most of the Western world to the September 11 disaster and continuing threat of terrorism has been a diminution of differences and unity of action. The solutions to overcoming the threat have included increased intelligence about how the world works, as well as greater understanding of and respect for the differences among cultures. The solutions to our educational problems demand similar cohesiveness in purpose, intelligence, and action. Teachers, their leaders, politicians, parents, and other community entities can, together, solve the problems that as groups acting individually they cannot resolve. Figure E.1, by artist Hilda Epner, represents all of us, working together to ensure a better future for the coming generations.

References

Adler, M. (1982). *The Paideia proposal: An educational manifesto.* New York: Macmillan.

American Federation of Teachers. (1999). *Making standards matter 1999.* Washington, DC: Author.

Apple, M. (2001). Markets, standards, teaching and teacher education. *Journal of Teacher Education, 52*(3), 182-196.

Argyris, C. (1976). *Increasing leadership effectiveness.* New York: Wiley.

Associated Press. (2001, September 23). Lawmakers move ahead on education. *[Rockland County, NY] Journal News,* p. A3.

Ball, D. L. (2000). Bridging practices: Intertwining content and pedagogy in teaching and learning to teach. *Journal of Teacher Education, 51*(3), 241-247.

Ball, D. L., & Cohen, D. K. (1996). Reform by the book: What is—or might be— the role of curriculum materials in teacher learning and instructional reform. *Educational Researcher, 25*(9), 6-8, 14.

Barksdale-Ladd, M. A., & Thomas, K. F. (2000). What's at stake in high-stakes testing: Teachers and parents speak out. *Journal of Teacher Education, 51*(5), 384-397.

Barton, P. (2001). *Achievement and reducing gaps: Reporting progress toward goals for academic achievement.* Washington, DC: National Education Goals Panel.

Bennis, W., & Nanus, B. (1985). *Leaders: The strategies for taking charge.* New York: Harper & Row.

Bert, A. (2001, May 17). Rally rips state exams. *[Rockland County, NY] Journal News,* p. A1.

Biederman, M. (2001, August 22). From headache to scholastic magnet. *New York Times,* p. B9.

Brookhart, S. M. (1999). Response to Delandshere and Petrosky's assessment of complex performances: Limitations of key measurement assumptions. *Educational Researcher, 28*(3), 25-28.

Cochran-Smith, M. (2000). Gambling on the future. *Journal of Teacher Education, 51*(4), 259-261.

Cochran-Smith, M. (2001). Teacher education at the turn of the century. *Journal of Teacher Education, 51*(3), 163-165.

Corcoran, T., & Goertz, M. (1995). Instructional capacity and high performance standards. *Educational Researcher, 24*(9), 27-31.

Council of Chief State School Officers. (1995). *State collaborative on assessment and student standards year-end report.* Washington, DC: Author.

Cronbach, L. J. (1963). Evaluation for course improvement. *Teachers College Record, 65,* 672-683.

Darling-Hammond, L. (1990). Instructional policy into practice: The power of the bottom over the top. *Educational Evaluation and Policy Analysis, 12*(3), 233-241.

Darling-Hammond, L. (Ed.). (1994). *Professional development schools: Integrated professional development-improving learning.* New York: Teachers College Press.

de Groot, C. (2000). Marshmallow peeps: Fostering a K-12 connection. *New York State Mathematics Teacher's Journal, 51*(1), 21-26.

Delandshere, G., & Petrosky, A. R. (1998). Assessment of complex performances: Limitations of key measurement assumptions, *Educational Researcher, 27*(2), 14-24.

Dewey, J. E. (1940). *Education today.* New York: Jan Rees Press.

Dewey, J. E. (1950). *Reconstruction in philosophy.* New York: Mentor Books. (Original work published 1920)

Dewey, J. E. (1973). Education as a social function. In S. D. Sieber & D. E. Wilder (Eds.), *The school in society.* New York: Free Press. (Original work published 1916)

Donohue, T. (1993). Finding the way: Structure, time and culture in school improvement. *Phi Delta Kappan, 74*(12), 298-305.

Durkheim, E. (1973). Education: Its nature and role. In S. D. Sieber & D. E. Wilder (Eds.), *The school in society* (pp. 11-27). New York: Free Press. (Original work published 1956)

Edmonds, R. R. (1983). Programs of school improvement: An overview. *Educational Leadership, 40*(4), 4-11.

Educational Testing Service. (1998). *Does it compute? The relationship between educational technology and student achievement in mathematics.* Princeton, NJ: Educational Testing Service.

Egeland, P. (1997). Pulleys, planes and student performance. *Educational Leadership, 54*(4), 41-45.

Fennema, E., Carpenter, T. P., Jacobs, V. R., Franke, M. L., & Levi, L. W. (1998). A longitudinal study of gender differences in young children's mathematical thinking. *Educational Researcher, 27*(5), 6-11.

Firestone, W. A., Fitz, J., & Broadfoot, P. (1999). Power, learning and legitimation: Assessment implementation across levels in the United States and the United Kingdom. *American Educational Research Journal, 36*(4), 759-793.

Flannery, P. (2001, September 7). Retooled AIMS contract boosts costs, expectation. *Arizona Republic,* pp. A1, B4.

Friedman, S. J. (2000). How much of a problem? A reply to Ingersoll's "The problem of underqualified teachers in American secondary schools." *Educational Researcher, 29*(5), 18-20.

Fullan, M. (1994, October 28). Managing Change. Paper presented at the meeting of the New York State Association for Supervision and Curriculum Development, Suffern, New York.

Gardner, H. (1993). *Multiple intelligences: The theory in practice.* New York: Basic Books.

Gerstner, L. V. (2001, October 9). Paper presented at the National Education Summit, Palisades, New York. Retrieved January 15, 2002, from www.ibm.com/lvg/1009.phtml

Gilman, D. A., & Lanman-Givens, B. (2001). Where have all the principals gone? *Educational Leadership, 58*(8), 72-74.

Ginsburg, H. P., Posner, J., & Russell, R. (1981). The development of knowledge concerning written arithmetic. *International Journal of Psychology, 16,* 13-34.

Glasser, W. (1986). *Control theory in the classroom.* New York: Harper & Row.

Glatthorn, A. (2000). *The principal as curriculum leader.* Thousand Oaks, CA: Corwin.

Goldenberg, C., Gallimore, R., Reese, L., & Garnier, H. (2001). Cause or effect? A longitudinal study of immigrant Latino parents' aspirations and expectations, and their children's school performance. *American Educational Research Journal, 38*(3), 547-582.

Goldhaber, D. D. (1999). School choice: An examination of the empirical evidence on achievement, parental decision making and equity. *Educational Researcher, 28*(9), 16-25.

Goodnough, A. (2001a, June 14). Strain of fourth-grade tests drives off veteran teachers. *New York Times,* p. A1.

Goodnough, A. (2001b, June 18). Interstate competition for teachers from aboard. *New York Times,* p. B10.

Goodnough, A. (2001c, July 7). Again, many empty seats in summer school classes. *New York Times,* pp. B1, B5.

Goodnough, A. (2002, January 26). New York City school board elections postponed. *New York Times,* p. B2.

Goodson, I. F. (1992). Sponsoring the teachers voice: Teachers' lives and teacher development. In A. Hargreaves & M. Fullan (Eds.), *Understanding teacher development.* London, UK: Cassell.

Gowen, A. (2001, September 11). All-day kindergarten boosts reading: 1-year Montgomery study reveals benefits for "high-risk" students. *Washington Post,* p. B1.

Grayson, D. A., & Martin, M. D. (2000). *Generating expectations for student achievement (GESA): An equitable approach to educational excellence.* Earlham, IA: Gray Mill Publications.

Hansen, K. H. (1967). Planning for changes in education. In E. Morphet & C. Ryan (Eds.), *Designing education for the future* (pp. 24-25). New York: Citation Press.

Hartocollis, A. (2001, October 30). Scarsdale warned not to boycott state tests. *New York Times,* p. A3.

Haycock, K. (2001). Closing the achievement gap. *Educational Leadership, 58*(6), 6-12.

Hayward, E. (2000, May 5). MCAS opponents hold rally in hub. *Boston Herald,* p. 5.

Hayward, E. (2001, September 25). Appeals process blueprint to go to ed. board. *Boston Herald,* p. 21.

Henrique, D. B., & Steinberg, J. (2001, May 5). Right answer, wrong score: Test flaws take toll. *New York Times,* pp. 1, 34-35.

Hill, H. (2001). Policy is not enough: Language and the interpretation of standards. *American Educational Research Journal, 38*(2), 289-318.

Hill, R. B., & Somers, A. (1996). A process for initiating change: Developing technology goals for a college of education. *Journal of Teacher Education, 47*(4), 300-306.

Hirsch, E. D. (1996). *The schools we need: And why we don't have them.* New York: Doubleday.

Hirsch, E. D. (2001). Seeking breadth and depth in the curriculum. *Educational Leadership, 59*(2), 22-29.

Holloway, L. (2001, October 2). Increasingly, the principal is a newcomer. *New York Times,* pp. D1, D5.

Holmes Group. (1995). *Tomorrow's schools of education.* East Lansing, MI: Author.

Horowitz, R. (1995). A 75-year legacy on assessment: Reflections from an interview with Ralph Tyler. *Journal of Educational Research, 89*(2), 68-75.

House, E. R. (1996). A framework for appraising educational reforms. *Educational Researcher, 25*(7), 6-14.

Huberman, M., & Miles, M. (1984). *Innovation up close.* New York: Plenum.

Huberman, M., & Miles, M. (1986). Rethinking the quest for school improvement: Some findings from the DESSI study. In A. Lieberman (Ed.), *Rethinking school improvement* (pp. 96-111). New York: Teachers College Press.

Hyde, J. S., & Jaffe, S. (1998). Perspectives from social and feminist psychology. *Educational Researcher, 27*(5), 14-16.

Ingersoll, R. M. (1999). The problem of under-qualified teachers in American secondary schools. *Educational Researcher, 28*(2), 26-37.

Ingersoll, R. M. (2001). Teacher turnover and teacher shortages: An organizational analysis. *American Educational Research Journal, 38*(3), 499-534.

Johnson, D. W., & Johnson, R. T. (1989). *Cooperation and competition: Theory and research.* Edina, MN: Interaction.

Kahlenberg, R. D. (2000). The new economic: School desegregation. *Educational Leadership, 7*(57), 16-19.

Kane, T. J., & Staiger, D. O. (2001, August 13). Rigid rules will damage schools. *New York Times,* p. A17.

Kirst, M. W. (1995). Recent research in intergovernmental relations in education. *Educational Researcher, 24*(9), 18-22.

Lave, J. (1977). Cognitive consequences of traditional apprenticeship training in West Africa. *Anthropology and Education Quarterly, 8,* 177-180.

Lehmann, S., & Spring, E. (1996). High academic standards and school reform: Education leaders speak out. In *Pre-summit briefing materials, 1996 Education Summit.* Palisades, New York: Governors Commission for New Standards.

Lerman, S. (1996). Intersubjectivity in mathematics learning: A challenge to the radical constructivist paradigm? *Journal for Research in Mathematics Education, 27*(2), 133-150.

Lieberman, A. (1996). Creating learning communities. *Educational Leadership, 54*(3), 51-55.

Lieberman, A. (2000). Networks as learning communities: Shaping the future of teacher development. *Journal of Teacher Education, 51*(3), 221-227.

Lieberman, A., & Miller, L. (1986). School improvement: Themes and variations. In A. Lieberman (Ed.), *Rethinking school improvement* (pp. 96-111). New York: Teachers College Press.

Lieberman, A., & Miller, L. (1990). Restructuring schools: What matters and what works. *Phi Delta Kappan, 71,* 759-764.

Linn, M., Lewis, C., Tsuchida, I., & Songer, N. B. (2000). Beyond fourth-grade science: Why do U.S. and Japanese students diverge? *Educational Researcher, 29*(3), 4-14.

Linn, R. L. (2000). Assessment and accountability. *Educational Researcher, 29*(2), 4-16.

Little, J. W. (1993). Teachers' professional development in a climate of reform. *Educational Evaluation and Policy Analysis, 15*(2), 129-151.

Lortie, D. C. (1975). *Schoolteacher.* Chicago: University of Chicago Press.

McCaslin, M. (1996). The problem of problem representation: The summit's conception of student. *Educational Researcher, 25*(8), 13-15.

McGuire, K. (2000). Agora: The impact of high-stakes testing. *Journal of Teacher Education, 51*(4), 289-292.

Mclain, D. L. (2001, March 7). Computer programmers needed, women please apply. *New York Times,* p. G1.

McNeil, L. (2000). *Contradictions of school reform: Educational costs of standardized testing.* New York: Routledge.

McTighe, J. (1996). What happens between assessments? *Educational Leadership, 54*(4), 6-12.

Meisels, S. J. (1996/1997). Using work sampling in authentic assessments. *Educational Leadership, 54*(4), 60-65.

Mercer, P. (2001, April 28). A mandate to force computer expertise. *New York Times,* p. B8.

Montgomery County Public Schools. (2001, June 25). *Schools Continue Well Above National Average and Kindergarten Study Shows More Potential as Higher Targets on Tests are Recommended.* Retrieved February 2, 2002, from coldfusion. mcps.k12.md.us/cfms/departments/info/pressreleases/detail.cfm?id=524

Moss, P. A., & Schutz, A. (2001). Educational standards, assessment and the search for consensus. *American Educational Research Journal, 38*(1), 37-70.

Mosle, S. (1996, September 8). Scores count. *New York Times.*

Mullis, I. V. S., Martin, M. O., Gonzalez, E. J., Gregory, K. D., Garden, R. A., O'Connor, K. M., Chrostowski, S. J., & Smith, T. A. (2000). *TIMSS 1999: International mathematics report.* Chestnut Hill, MA: Boston College.

National Center for Education Statistics (NCES). (1999). The condition of education 1999. Retrieved April 16, 2002, from http://nces.ed.gov/pubs99/condition99/scc-1.html

National Commission on Excellence in Education. (1983). *A nation at risk.* Washington, DC: United States Department of Education.

National Commission on Mathematics and Science Teaching for the 21st Century. (2000). *Before it's too late.* Washington, DC: U.S. Department of Education.

National Council for the Social Studies. (1994). *Curriculum standards for the social studies: Expectations of excellence.* Washington, DC: Author.

National Council of Teachers of Mathematics. (2000). *Principles and standards for school mathematics.* Reston, VA: Author.

National Council of Teachers of Mathematics, Commission on Standards for School Mathematics. (1989). *Curriculum and evaluation standards for school mathematics.* Reston, VA: Author.

National Education Commission on Time and Learning. (1994). *Prisoners of time.* Washington, DC: U.S. Government Printing Office.

National Research Council. (1996). *National science education standards.* Washington, DC: National Academy Press.

National Research Council, Commission on Behavioral and Social Sciences and Education. (2000). *Eager to learn: Educating our pre-schoolers.* Washington, DC: National Academy Press.

Natriello, G. (1996). Diverting attention from conditions in American schools. *Educational Researcher, 25*(8), 7-9.

No Child Left Behind Act of 2001. (2002). Retrieved February 1, 2002, from www.whitehouse.gov/infocus/education

Noddings, N. (1998). Perspectives from feminist philosophy. *Educational Researcher, 27*(5), 17-18.

Ornstein, A. C. (1975). The politics of accountability. *Clearing House, 49*(1), 5-10.

Owston, D. (1997). The World Wide Web: A technology to enhance learning? *Educational Researcher, 26*(2), 27-34.

Perkins, D. (1992). *Smart schools: Better thinking and learning for every child.* New York: Free Press.

Piaget, J. (1977). *The development of thought: Equilibration of cognitive structures.* New York: Viking.

Pintrich, P. R., Marx, R. W., & Boyle, R. A. (1993). Beyond cold conceptual change: The role of motivational beliefs and contextual factors in the process of conceptual change. *Review of Educational Research, 63*(2), 167-169.

Polya, G. (1956). How to solve it. In J. R. Newman (Ed.), *The world of mathematics* (Vol. 3, pp. 1980-1989). New York: Simon & Schuster. (Original work published 1945)

Popham, W. J. (2001). Teaching to the test. *Educational Leadership, 58*(6), 16-20.

Popkewitz, T. S. (2000). The denial of change in educational change: Systems of ideas in the construction of national policy and evaluation. *Educational Researcher, 29*(1), 17-29.

Raspberry, W. (2001, August 25). Focus on children, not leaders. *[Rockland County, NY] Journal News,* p. B5.

Reitzug, U. C. (1994). A case study of empowering principal behavior. *American Educational Research Journal, 31*(2), 283-307.

Resnick, L. B., & Resnick, D. (1989). *Tests as standards of achievement in schools: The uses of standardized tests in American education.* Princeton, NJ: Educational Testing Service.

Rice, E. H. (2002). *Journal of Teacher Education, 53*(1), 55-67.

Riehl, C. (2000). The principal's role in creating inclusive schools for diverse students: A review of normative, empirical, and critical literature on the practice of educational administration. *Review of Educational Research, 70*(1), 55-81.

Rossi, R. (2001, November 6). State issues harder tests for new teachers. *Chicago Sun Times,* p. 1.

Rothstein, R. (2001, July 18). Who puts the standards in standardized tests? *New York Times,* p. B9.

Salomon, J. (2001, September 3). Public education's rocky road. *New York Times,* p. E1.

Sarason, S. B. (1972). *The creation of settings and the future societies.* San Francisco: Jossey-Bass.

Sarason, S. (1990). *The predictable failure of educational reform.* San Francisco: Jossey-Bass.

Sarason, S. (1993). *The case for change.* San Francisco: Jossey-Bass.

Schmidt, W., McNight, C., Cogan, L., Jakwerth, P., & Houang, R. (1999). *Facing the consequences: Using TIMSS for a closer look at U.S. mathematics and science education.* Dordrecht, The Netherlands: Kluwer.

Schoenfeld, A. (1999). Looking toward the 21st century: Challenges of educational theory and practice. *Educational Researcher, 28*(7), 4-14.

Shepard, L. A. (2000). The role of assessment in a learning culture. *Educational Researcher, 29*(7), 4-14.

Sindelar, P. T., & Rosenberg, M. S. (2000). Serving too many masters: The proliferation of ill-conceived and contradictory policies and practices in teacher education. *Journal of Teacher Education, 51*(3), 183-193.

Smith, M. L., & Fey, P. (2000). Validity and accountability in high-stakes testing. *Journal of Teacher Education, 51*(5), 334-344.

Smylie, M. A. (1996). From bureaucratic control to building human capital: The importance of teacher learning in education reform. *Educational Researcher, 25*(9), 9-11.

Solomon, P. G. (1980). Does career education make a difference? *The Science Teacher, 47*(8), 32-35.

Solomon, P. G. (1995). *No small feat: Taking time for change.* Thousand Oaks, CA: Corwin.

Solomon, P. G. (1998). *The curriculum bridge: From standards to actual classroom practice.* Thousand Oaks, CA: Corwin.

Solomon, P. G. (2000). *The math we need to "know" and "do": Content standards for the elementary and middle grades.* Thousand Oaks, CA: Corwin.

Song, M., & Ginsburg, H. (1987). The development of informal and formal mathematical thinking in Korean and U.S. children. *Child Development, 58,* 1272-1285.

Sowder, J. T. (1998). Perspectives from mathematics education. *Educational Researcher, 27*(5), 12-13.

Spady, W., & Marshall, K. (1990). *Vail leadership seminars.* Santa Cruz, CA: High Success Program.

Spillane, J., Halverson, R., & Diamond, J. S. (2001). Investigating school leadership practice: A distributive perspective. *Educational Leadership, 30*(3), 23-28.

Steffe, L. P., & D'Ambrosio, B. (1995). Toward a working model of constructivist teaching: A reaction to Simon. *Journal of Mathematics Teaching, 26*(2), 146-159.

Steinberg, J. (2001, October 10). National education talks languish in shadow of war. *New York Times,* p. A15.

Stout, R. T. (1997). Staff development policy: Fuzzy choices in an imperfect market. Retrieved February 2, 2002, from epaa.asu.edu/epaa/v4n2.html

Suter, L. (2000). Is student achievement immutable? Evidence from international studies on schooling and student achievement. *Review of Educational Research, 70*(4), 529-545.

Tannen, D. (1994, August 28). How to give orders to a man. *New York Times Magazine.* p. 46.

Tobias, S. (1994). Interest, prior knowledge, and learning. *Review of Educational Research, 64*(1), 37-54.

Tomlinson, C. A. (2000). Reconcilable differences: Standards-based teaching and differentiation. *Educational Leadership, 59*(1), 6-11.

Trotter, A. (1998). A question of effectiveness. In "Technology Counts '98," *Education Week* Special Report. Available online at www.edweek.org/reports/tc98/intro/in-n.htm

Tyler, R. W. (1949). *Basic principles of curriculum and instruction.* Chicago: University of Chicago Press.

U.S. Department of Commerce, Economics and Statistics Administration, National Telecommunications and Information Administration. (2000, October). *Falling through the net: Toward digital inclusion: A report on Americans' access to technology tools.* Retrieved February 2, 2002, from www.esa.doc.gov/fttn00.htm

U.S. Department of Education. (1991). *America 2000: An education strategy.* Washington, DC: Author.

U.S. Department of Education. (2001, August 2). *Prepared Remarks of U.S. Secretary of Education Rod Paige: The Nation's Report Card—Mathematics 2000.* Retrieved February 1, 2002, from www.ed.gov/PressReleases/08-2001/08022001.html

University of the State of New York. (1997). *Math, science and technology resource guide.* Albany: Author.

University of the State of New York. (2000). *New York State testing program: Mathematics scoring guide.* Albany: Author.

Valencia, S., & Place, N. (1994). Portfolios: A process for enhancing teaching and learning. *The Reading Teacher, 47*(8), 666-669.

Van Lehn, K. (1986). Arithmetic procedures are induced from examples. In J. Hiebert (Ed.), *Conceptual and procedural knowledge: The case of mathematics* (pp. 133-179). Hillsdale, NJ: Lawrence Erlbaum.

Von Glasersfeld, E. (1990). Environment and communication. In L. P. Steffe & T. Wood (Eds.), *Transforming children's mathematics education: International perspectives* (pp. 30-38). Hillsdale, NJ: Lawrence Erlbaum.

Vygotsky, L. S. (1978). *Mind in society: The development of higher psychological processes.* M. Cole, V. J. Steiner, S. Scribner, & E. Souberman (Eds. & Trans.). Cambridge, MA: Harvard University Press.

Wasser, J. D., & Bresler, L. (1996). Working in the interpretive zone: Conceptualizing collaboration in qualitative research teams. *Educational Researcher, 25*(5), 5-15.

Webb, L. D., Metha, A., & Jordan, K. F. (1996). *Foundations of American education.* Englewood Cliffs, NJ: Merrill.

Weiner, R. (2001, October 10). Education summit focuses on formulas for success. *[Rockland County, NY] Journal News,* p. B1.

Weinstein, R. S., Madison, S. M., & Kuklinsky, M. R. (1995). Raising expectations in schooling: Obstacles and opportunities. *American Educational Research Journal, 32*(1), 121-161.

Wentzel, K. R. (1993). Motivation and achievement in early adolescence: The role of multiple classroom goals. *Journal of Early Adolescence, 13,* 4-20.

Wertsch, J. V. (1979). From social interaction to higher psychological process: A clarification and application of Vygotsky's theory. *Human Development, 22*(1), 1-22.

Wiggins, G. (1995). Standards, not standardization: Evoking quality student work. In A. C. Ornstein & L. S. Behar (Eds.), *Contemporary issues in curriculum* (pp. 187-195). Boston: Allyn & Bacon.

Wilgoren, J. (2001, July). State school chiefs fret over U.S. plan to require testing. *New York Times,* p. A1.

Wilson, D. M. (2001a, July 15). Federal school testing opposed. *[Rockland County, NY] Journal News,* p. A1.

Wilson, D. M. (2001b, October 11). Education summit calls for more testing. *[Rockland County, NY] Journal News,* p. B1.

Wilson, D. M., & Weiner, R. (2001, October 10). Education called key to defense. *[Rockland County, NY] Journal News,* p. B1.

Windschitl, M. (1998). The WWW and classroom research: What path should we take? *Educational Researcher, 27*(1), 28-33.

Woodward, J., & Rieth, H. (1997). A historical review of technology research in special education. *Review of Educational Research, 67*(4), 503-536.

Zeichner, K. M., & Schulte, A. K. (2001). What we know and don't know from peer-reviewed research about alternative teacher certification programs. *Journal of Teacher Education, 52*(4), 266-282.

Zernike, K. (2001, June 17). Schools' difficult search for "just right" standards. *New York Times,* p. B1.

Index

**CORWIN
PRESS**

The Corwin Press logo—a raven striding across an open book—represents the happy union of courage and learning. We are a professional-level publisher of books and journals for K-12 educators, and we are committed to creating and providing resources that embody these qualities. Corwin's motto is "Success for All Learners."